Contents

By matching up the guides at the edge of this page with the marks opposite them along the edge of the book, you can quickly turn to the unit containing the material you want.

Reference Manual

For Office Personnel

6th Edition

Clifford R. House

President Emeritus
Cincinnati Technical College

Kathie Sigler

Dean for Administration and Professor
Miami-Dade Community College

K45U

Published by

SOUTH-WESTERN PUBLISHING CO.

CINCINNATI   WEST CHICAGO, ILL.   DALLAS   PELHAM MANOR, N.Y.   PALO ALTO, CALIF.

ISBN: 0-538-11452-5
Library of Congress Catalog Card Number: 78-58013

5 6 7 8 9 10 11 12 13 14 K 4 3 2 1 0 9 8 7

PREFACE

Reference Manual for Office Personnel, Sixth Edition, is a useful reference for anyone who writes, edits, or processes written words (particularly in a business environment), and an effective text for anyone who is preparing for a job in today's business office. Newly available **Study Guides** should be particularly helpful for those wishing to test their knowledge of a particular area and measure their increased knowledge after study and discussion of the information presented in this Manual.

While the fundamentals included in the previous editions have been retained, the Sixth Edition has been *reorganized* and *rewritten* to reflect changes in style and emerging preferences on the part of the previous editions' users.

Changes in style range from the elimination of sexism in the language to revision of the ZIP Code system; responses to users' suggestions range from a unit on "Getting the Job/Getting Ahead" to the addition of **Study Guides**.

The new spiral binding allows for easy access to all pages, while at the same time permitting the opened Manual to lie flat on a desk for continued reference. In addition, the thumb index provides immediate access to all major sections. A carefully structured system of headings and paragraph numbers constitutes a second and more detailed system of access; a comprehensive, well cross-referenced index helps locate more elusive information. Notes and cross-references also are included in the text whenever additional information is needed.

Rules and conventions are expressed in clear, easy-to-follow language, with examples used generously to aid understanding. New, easy-to-read type styles combined with a second color emphasis also contribute to a format that is efficient, convenient, and attractive.

Major improvements include:

UNIT

1 **"Getting the Job/Getting Ahead."** This new unit is included at the request of business educators and office personnel interested in information on finding, getting, and keeping a job. Also included are tips on career advancement.

2 **"Grammar."** This unit has been expanded to allow for coverage of additional material, while at the same time simplified in rules and examples presented. New in this section are easy-to-use suggestions for elimination of sexism in business writing.

3 **"Punctuation."** Unit 3 has been increased by one-third, permitting the treatment of additional uses of punctuation.

4&5 **"Capitalization"** and **"Abbreviations."** Both units have been updated to include the most recent preferences of the business office.

6 **"Word Division."** Clear, easy-to-understand rules and conventions make producing attractive typewritten pages easy.

7 **"Numbers."** This reorganized unit includes three different styles for writing numbers: general, technical, and formal.

8 **"Business Mathematics."** This unit presents a new, straight-to-the-point treatment of percentage, discounts, markups, and the metric system.

9 **"Typing Basics."** Unit 9 contains a complete review of basic typing information, including horizontal and vertical centering, tabulation, and proofreading. A *new*, comprehensive section on corrections covers the latest in correction techniques and choices.

10&11 **"Letters/Memos"** and *"Reports/Manuscripts."* Both units have been modernized to include current practices in the business office. Examples have been expanded for ease of reference.

12 **"Envelopes/Mail/Telephone."** Unit 12 is a guide to using external communication systems available to the business office.

13 **"Reference Books."** This unit has been expanded to include more suggested references for particular problem areas brought to our attention by Manual users.

Please remember that recognized authorities do not always agree on matters of style or grammatical usage. When concensus does exist, it is reflected in this Manual. When preferences differ, this Manual represents what seems to be the majority opinion and, in many instances, indicates that more than one treatment is acceptable.

Many of the improvements in this Sixth Edition were made at the suggestion of teachers and office workers. We are grateful for their contributions and encourage all users to continue to offer suggestions for making this Manual a more effective resource.

CLIFFORD R. HOUSE

KATHIE SIGLER

UNIT 1
Getting the Job ▪ Getting Ahead

This is for those of you who are, or soon will be, job hunting. Most people change occupations several times during their lifetimes. Therefore, the ability to find and make the most of job opportunities is a valuable skill well worth learning and improving.

101   A Personal Survey

Before you can convince a prospective employer of your qualifications for a position, you must be able to recognize them yourself. Take a *personal survey* of your strengths and weaknesses. Make a list of the strengths you could most use to sell yourself as the best candidate for a job. Keep your strengths in mind during job interviews. Doing so will help you make the interviewer aware of your qualifications for the job. Identified weaknesses should be targeted as future growth areas.

Next, ask yourself what kind of a job you want. Be specific. The answer to this question is more than "I want to be a secretary." What kind of company do you want to employ you? If you have always been fascinated by advertising and public relations, you may want to concentrate on secretarial jobs in this field. Do you enjoy meeting people? If not, you may want to avoid a job in which some of your duties involve greeting the public. Think carefully about your personal likes and dislikes in selecting a job. Once you get the job, you are more likely to get ahead if you like your work. Strictly speaking, job satisfaction may be essential to career advancement.

Finally, consider the opportunities for promotion in the types of job openings you select. Talk to counselors, teachers, friends working in the same field, and others in positions to know about opportunities for advancement in the career areas that interest you.

Once you know yourself—your strengths and weaknesses, the career areas that interest you most, and the opportunities for advancement on the job—you are ready to match your interests and skills with available jobs.

102   Finding Available Jobs

Job opportunities should be available to all—regardless of factors such as sex, race, religion, creed, age, or physical disability. There are two approaches you can use for finding job vacancies. The first approach involves researching areas where job vacancies are advertised or posted:

- Help-Wanted Ads from the Classified Sections of Newspapers

- High School/College Placement Offices or Bulletin Boards

- Employment Agencies: State or Private

- Periodicals, Magazines, Professional and Trade Journals, Yearbooks for the career field of your choice. You can usually find these in your local library.

Read through job opening notices to find vacancies that will match your personal skills and interests. If you select a private employment agency, make sure it is clearly understood who pays the agency fee should you get the job. It is wise to avoid employment agencies requiring advance fees. Once you have found job openings that interest you, the next steps are to write an application letter and to prepare your resume.

The second approach to finding job openings involves contacting prospective employers to see if there are any job vacancies. This process is simplified through the following:

Friends and acquaintances. Check with your family, friends, and acquaintances to determine what possible job vacancies they may have heard about.

Business news items. Watch your local newspaper for announcements of new companies moving into your area, local companies expanding, or new contracts awarded. All of these situations could create job vacancies.

Yellow Pages. The Yellow Pages of your local telephone directory are a good source of employment information. Contact companies doing business in the career areas that appeal to you.

Personnel offices. Call or visit the personnel offices of local companies to find out about current job vacancies.

Job openings are often discovered through this second approach by writing a job inquiry/application letter to potential employers.

103   Letter of Application

The *letter of application* accompanies the personal data sheet to the prospective employer. The main purpose of the application letter is to persuade the reader to invite you for an interview. There are two types of application letters you may use. The first is a letter of application used to apply for a specific advertised or posted job vacancy. (See Illustration 1-1.) The second is a *job inquiry/application letter* used to apply for a job that *may be* available. (See Illustration 1-2.)

Whether you are applying for an identified job vacancy, or trying to determine if job vacancies exist, the letter of application should accomplish the following:

1. *Attract Attention.* Put yourself in the position of the person reading, perhaps, 50 application letters. To have your letter "stand out from the rest," you must find a unique way to tie together the needs of the company and your own talents and abilities in a way that will be remembered. Use the first paragraph of the letter to attract attention to your application. Refer to the first paragraphs of Illustrations 1-1 and 1-2 for examples; then use your own imagination to create attention-getting first paragraphs that will work for you.

2. *Emphasize Your Qualifications.* The middle portion of the application letter (between the attention-getting first paragraph and the action-producing concluding paragraph) should emphasize the qualifications detailed in your personal data sheet. Picture yourself standing over the shoulder of the person reading your data sheet. Think of those parts of your personal data sheet you would like to reach down and point out to the reader as examples of how you are best qualified to fill a job vacancy. These are the areas that you should highlight in your letter of application.

3. *Request Action.* In the final paragraph of your application letter, ask for action or response. The action you request depends on what you know about the selection process. If you know interviews and final selection will be conducted by the personnel manager, you could say that you will call next week to ask for an interview. If you know, however, that a selection committee will be used to make recommendations of finalists, you could ask that the committee contact you for any additional information needed.

ILLUSTRATION 1-1.   *Sample Letter of Application Using Block Style and Mixed Punctuation*

19314 Chapel Avenue
Detroit, MI 48219-3621
January 15, 19--

Ms. Ileana Gonzalez, Manager
Personnel Department
Chevrolet Motor Division
General Motors Corporation
3044 W. Grand Boulevard
Detroit, MI 48202-3726

Dear Ms. Gonzalez:

An enthusiastic, organized, and personable individual with secretarial experience at the executive level is needed for the administrative assistant position advertised in the Detroit News
on January 10, 19--. I am eager to learn and enthusiastic about
an opportunity to work as an administrative assistant with the
Chevrolet Motor Division.

Highlighted here are some of my qualifications from the attached
personal data sheet:

1. A.S. Degree in Secretarial Careers from Lake Pierce Community
   College. Specific secretarial skills include 120 wpm
   shorthand, 60 wpm typing, and the ability to operate office
   machines including electronic calculators, transcribing
   machines, and automatic typewriters.

2. Organization. While working as executive secretary for the
   sales manager at the Park Shelton Hotel, I organized the
   convention inquiry and follow-up system still in use at the
   hotel.

3. Personable. My job responsibilities at the Park Shelton
   Hotel also include meeting the public on a daily basis,
   solving convention problems unanticipated in convention
   planning, and coordinating each convention effort among
   all the departments of the hotel.

4. Secretarial Experience. My part-time secretarial experience
   while in high school and college prepared me for the secretarial position at the hotel. The total of four years
   secretarial experience I now have should prepare me well for
   the administrative assistant position at Chevrolet Motor
   Division.

Ms. Ileana Gonzalez
Page 2
January 15, 19--

Ms. Gonzalez, I sincerely appreciate your serious consideration
of my application and would welcome the opportunity to talk with
you. I will call your office Thursday to arrange an appointment.

Sincerely,

Marcia Stringer

Ms. Marcia Stringer

Enclosure

ILLUSTRATION 1-2

Sample Job Inquiry/Application Letter Using Modified Block Style and Open Punctuation

```
                                    19314 Chapel Avenue
                                    Detroit, MI  48219-3621
                                    January 15, 19--


Personnel Department
First National Bank
1001 Woodward Avenue
Detroit, MI  48226-3780

Ladies and Gentlemen

Is your bank in the market for a secretary who can:

... type at 60 wpm

... take shorthand at 120 wpm

... operate office machines?

If so, I am just the secretary for you!

While completing my A.S. Degree in Secretarial Careers at Lake
Pierce Community College, I developed these skills.  I also
received an "A" grade in a course called "Banking & Finance."
I enjoyed this course and would like to continue to learn about
the banking industry through employment with your bank.

My present job with the Park Shelton Hotel has helped me develop
an ability to work well with all kinds of people.  My duties
include meeting the public on a daily basis, solving convention
problems unanticipated in convention planning, and coordinating
each convention effort among all departments of the hotel.

I would appreciate your serious consideration of my enclosed data
sheet and welcome the opportunity to talk with you further about
employment possibilities at the First National Bank.  Please call
me at 537-5885 at your earliest convenience to set up an appoint-
ment.  I'll look forward to hearing from you.

                         Sincerely

                         Marcia Stringer

                         Ms. Marcia Stringer

Enclosure
```

DO'S AND DON'TS OF APPLICATION LETTERS

- **DO** consider the use of good quality bond paper for both your letter of application and your resume. Cream-colored, beige, or grey paper is recommended to make your application stand out from others.

- DO type your application letter, using standard business letter form. (Refer to Unit 10 of this manual for a review of business letters.)

- DON'T use letterhead stationery from your present employer to apply for a job with another company.

- DON'T send your application letter with errors or obvious corrections. Proofread carefully and check all questionable spelling.

104   The Personal Data Sheet

Like the application letter, the personal data sheet opens the door to the job interview. The *personal data sheet*—sometimes called a *vita, resume,* or *dossier*—provides a prospective employer with a summary of all of your qualifications for a particular job.

While there is a specific format usually followed in data sheet writing, the format and content of a personal data sheet may be tailored to emphasize your qualifications for a particular job. This means that to apply for a job opening in banking, you may wish to stress the part of your education and experience dealing with banking and numbers. Application for a different job in a word processing department, however, would call for a different emphasis within the data sheet. Also, since the personal data sheet and application letter are probably the employer's first (and perhaps only) experience with you, care should be taken to make the data sheet attractive in style and format; it should contain no typing errors or messy corrections and should present as accurate and positive a picture of your qualifications as possible.

If you have decided to use cream-colored, beige, or grey paper for your letter of application, the personal data sheet should be typed on the same paper. Using colored bond paper of this type will help your data sheet stand out from a stack of hundreds that may be received.

Personal data sheets are always typed and usually organized into the following parts:

Heading and personal information. Most data sheets begin with the title *Personal Data Sheet,* followed by the applicant's name, address, and telephone number. (See Illustration 1-3.) A new trend, however, is to include a job objective—either as part of the title:

QUALIFICATIONS OF JAMES CLAYBOURNE FOR EMPLOYMENT AS
SECRETARY FOR CUAN BINDING COMPANY

or as a separate category following the heading and personal information:

JOB OBJECTIVE: Executive Secretary

ILLUSTRATION 1-3

Sample Personal Data Sheet

```
                    PERSONAL DATA SHEET

                    Marcia B. Stringer

                    19314 Chapel Avenue
                    Detroit, MI  48219-3621
                      (313) 537-5885

JOB OBJECTIVE:                      Executive Secretary

EDUCATION

A.S.       September, 19--, to     Lake Pierce Community College
           June, 19--              Miami, FL
                                   Secretarial Careers Major
                                   Degree Awarded:  June, 19--

                                   Occupational Skills:
                                       Typing 60 wpm
                                       Shorthand 120 wpm
                                       Office Machines
                                       Transcribing Machines
                                       Automatic Typewriters

Diploma    September, 19--, to     Henry Ford High School
           June, 19--              Detroit, MI
                                   Business Education Major
                                   Diploma:  June, 19--

WORK EXPERIENCE

July, 19--, to Present             Executive Secretary
                                   Park Shelton Hotel
                                   Detroit, MI

Summer, 19--, 19--                 Receptionist/Typist
                                   Reserve Insurance Company
                                   Detroit, MI

REFERENCES (with permission)

Mr. A. Starr Hull, Manager         Mrs. Elizabeth Forrester
Park Shelton Hotel                 Department Chairperson
8542 Woodward Avenue               Secretarial Careers Department
Detroit, MI  48202-3652            Lake Pierce Community College
(313) 535-7882                     Miami, FL  33132-1676
                                   (305) 577-6766
```

Carefully proofread well-known facts such as your address and telephone number. In the past, additional information such as birth date, birthplace, social security number, height and weight, marital status, number and ages of children, etc., have been included in this section. Legislation prohibiting discrimination in hiring, however, has made the inclusion of these items optional.

Education. List degrees earned (most recent first), dates attended school, educational institution awarding diploma or degree, city and state of school, educational major, and date degree was awarded. Optional information could include scholarships, academic honors, or a listing of occupational courses or skills (more important if you do not have much work experience).

Experience. List each job, dates worked (most recent first), job title, employer, and city and state of employment. Optional information could include names and addresses of supervisors and specific job duties and responsibilities.

Other optional categories. Depending on the type of job you are seeking, you may wish to include information from any of the following categories that might strengthen employment possibilities:

• References. Contact each reference used to obtain permission. Provide the name, job title, business address, and phone number for each reference.

• Related activities. Include items such as community activities, professional memberships, hobbies, and special interests.

• Military. If you have had military experience, list the branch of service, muster dates, rank, military occupation specialty, honors and awards.

• High school or college activities.

Your personal data sheet should be as brief as possible, while still providing all information to help you get that job. As your experience and education grow, your data sheet will increase in length. For additional data sheet pages, use this heading:

PERSONAL DATA SHEET
Your Name
Page 2

105   Completing Application Forms

When you call or visit a business to seek employment, you will usually be asked to fill out an *application form*. It is important that you fill out this form neatly and accurately. If possible, type it. If you must fill it out by hand, print the information. Follow the directions—watch for "last name first, first name, initial" and complete in that order. Fill in all blanks. If the question does not apply to you, either write "NA" in the blank for "not applicable" or draw a horizontal line in the space provided. Use your personal data sheet for handy reference on exact dates and addresses while filling out the application form. Make sure information given on the application and data sheet agree exactly. If asked for salary desired, provide a salary range instead of a specific amount. This will leave the salary issue open for discussion during the interview. Attach your personal data sheet to the completed application form.

106   The Interview

While an employer can judge your basic qualifications from your letter of application, personal data sheet, and completed application form, the *interview* is the occasion when an employer will judge your appearance, personality, attitudes, ability to communicate, and enthusiasm. The interview also gives you a chance to evaluate the potential job.

Before the interview. Learn all you can about the company interviewing you. Become familiar with the goods and services provided by the company to the community. Learn about current salaries for the same position with other companies, as well as employment benefits such as hospitalization, life insurance, vacation and sick leave, etc. Decide which of your personal qualities you want to emphasize during the interview and how they relate to the job opening. Ask family and friends for possible questions you might expect during the interview and practice possible answers. Write down questions you want to ask about the company, the job responsibilities, salary, and benefit information. Decide in advance what to wear. Remember, the best advice about what to wear for the interview *and* once you get the job is: DRESS, NOT FOR THE POSITION YOU DESIRE, BUT FOR THE ONE JUST ABOVE IT! Books providing research-based advice on dressing for the interview are listed in Unit 13, Reference Books, ¶ 1310 of this manual.

On the day of the interview. Plan ahead to give yourself plenty of time to get ready and to get to the interview. Before leaving home, make sure you know exactly how to get to the interview location.

During the interview. Try to relax. It is normal to be nervous, but try not to call attention to your nervousness by twisting your hands, etc. The interview will last approximately 20-30 minutes. Let the interviewer conduct the interview. Listen carefully to questions and provide more than yes and no answers. Look the interviewer in the eye and answer all questions honestly and frankly. If you do not understand a question, ask for clarification before attempting to answer it. Keep your final goal in mind—to sell yourself. Emphasize your good points and relate them to the vacant position. Do not criticize yourself, a teacher, or former employer. Ask your questions about the job at the end of the interview. Finally, if you are interested in working for this organization, let the interviewer know. Watch for clues that the interview is ending. The interviewer may ask you to schedule a test, inform you that a decision will be made within a certain period, offer you the job, etc. If you are offered the job, you can ask for a day or so to think it over.

107   Employment Tests

Employment tests are given by the prospective employer to obtain additional information for use in employee selection. General intelligence, math, typing, and shorthand tests are examples of employment tests. Sometimes an employer will accept a recent school certificate verifying typing or shorthand speed instead of requiring you to take these tests again. Take such certificates with you to the interview and testing situations.

Regardless of the type of employment test you will take, several suggestions can help you improve your test-taking potential:

1. Try to relax as much as possible.

2. Read the instructions carefully and ask questions if you do not understand the directions.

3. Divide your time among the sections of the test to make sure you have an idea of the time required for each.

4. Do not permit yourself to get stuck on any one question. Leave it and move along. Come back if you have time.

5. Don't change an answer unless you are *positive* your new answer is correct. Research shows that the more answers you change, the more likely you are to lower your score.

6. Write legibly! Don't lose points because your answer cannot be read.

7. Look for answers to harder questions in other test items.

You may also be required to take a physical examination for employment. Such exams are usually required for insurance purposes.

108   Follow-Up

It is a good idea to write a thank-you letter within a few days following the interview. Simply thank the interviewer for the time spent in the interview and indicate that you are sincerely interested in the job. This will also bring your name back to the mind of the interviewer as a prospective employee.

Take time to evaluate your performance. Make notes of what you would like to improve, and review these notes prior to your next job interview.

109   Keeping the Job—Moving Up in the Organization

Congratulations! You've got that job, and now you must plan to keep the job and look ahead to future advancement. Consider these steps:

1. When beginning a new position, remember that you cannot learn or accomplish everything at once.

   - Ask questions when you do not understand, *before* beginning a job.

   - Admit mistakes immediately. Go to your supervisor and discuss the error, taking the blame. Indicate you intend to be careful so that the same mistake does not occur again, and ask for advice and assistance on finding a solution to the mistake, if needed. You will be surprised at the cooperation you will receive—as well as the anger you will avoid—by pointing out and correcting your own mistake.

   - Do not continue any task that doesn't make sense to you. Check to make certain you are proceeding correctly.

2. Continue to grow on the job.

   - Take additional courses at your local college, university, high school, trade school, etc.

   - Join professional organizations:
     National Secretaries Association (NSA)
     National Association of Legal Secretaries (NALS)
     National Association of Educational Secretaries (NAES)
     American Association of Medical Assistants

   - Become a Certified Professional Secretary. The CPS rating indicates that the person has successfully passed an examination administered by the Institute for Certifying Secretaries of the National Secretaries Association (International). The CPS rating has brought professional recognition to secretaries and testifies to a broad background in the business field.

3. Join the company team.

   - Show your concern about the completion of any task, even if a rush job means working extra hours.

   - Demonstrate initiative by anticipating your employer's needs, obtaining information for your employer before being asked to do so, and making suggestions for the solution of office problems.

   - Build positive human relations with co-workers by always being pleasant and cooperative, volunteering to assist with high-priority projects, and remaining courteous during stressful situations.

   - Organize your work by setting up priorities, planning your day, creating forms or form letters for routine tasks, and maintaining an accurate office calendar.

- Set promotion goals. Once you decide on future promotion possibilities, take time to observe successful employees in similar positions. Notice how they dress, how they conduct themselves on the job, the way they relate to other workers, and how they handle stressful situations. Try similar behaviors yourself.

Following these suggestions will enable you to succeed on your present job and to make the most of future career possibilities. Good luck!

UNIT 2 *Grammar*

2

Grammar is the study of words—the way they function in sentences and the relationship of one to another. Grammatical guidelines provide a framework for communication. Effective communication is easier when we all group words together in sentences in the same way.

As you work, you will be judged by the skill with which you can communicate ideas. The ability to effectively communicate in business through letters, memos, and reports is a skill that can be learned and improved. A good beginning is a thorough understanding of the eight major parts of the speech—nouns, pronouns, verbs, adjectives, adverbs, conjunctions, prepositions, and interjections. These are the eight categories into which words are grouped, depending on the way they are used within a sentence.

Solutions to additional grammar questions can be found through the use of any of the books listed in Unit 13, Reference Books (see ¶ 1309).

NOUNS

201   *Nouns*, the most frequently used words, are used to identify someone or something. Nouns identify persons, places, things, or ideas.

Persons: Roberto, Miss Willie Mae Pinkney, women

Places: Miami, Walt Disney World, parks

Things: Golden Gate Bridge, novel, glass

Ideas: freedom, democracy

202   Common Nouns/Proper Nouns

There are two kinds of nouns, common nouns and proper nouns. A *common noun* names any one of a group or an entire group of persons, places, things, or ideas and is not capitalized. A *proper noun* names a particular person, place, thing, or idea and is always capitalized.

Common Nouns	*Proper Nouns*
professor	Dr. Anita Streit, Mr. Goldstein
country	United States of America, Italy
company	Alina Cordova Consultants, Inc.
	Thompson's Office Supplies
speech	Gettysburg Address

Nouns may be written in the *singular* (referring to one) or *plural* (more than one).

Singular	*Plural*
boy	boys
woman	women
worker	workers
church	churches
life	lives

Note: The plural forms of nouns are generally formed by adding *s* (as in *boys, workers*). Some nouns, however, form the plural according to different guidelines (as in *women, churches, lives*).

203   Compound Nouns

A *compound noun* consists of two or more words used as a single noun. Sometimes the words are

combined and written as one: firehouse

written as two or more words: post office

hyphenated: mother-in-law

Compound nouns do not follow any patterns. To check the spelling of a compound noun, consult your dictionary. If the word is not in your dictionary, treat it as two separate words.

When part of a company name is a compound noun, always follow the same style listed on the company's letterhead.

Compound nouns containing the words *man* or *men* traditionally have been used to refer to men and women alike. More recently, however, this usage has been criticized as discriminatory when applied to women. The fourth edition of the *Dictionary of*

Occupational Titles (DOT) has been revised to eliminate *all* sexual identifiers:

Mail*man* now becomes mail carrier.

This recent *DOT* edition also eliminates implied age bias in occupational titles:

Bus*boy* now becomes dining room attendant.

Suggested alternatives for commonly used compound nouns are listed below. For additional information, consult the *DOT*.

Avoid	*Use Instead*
man, men, mankind	people, person(s), human(s), individual(s), humanity
businessman	business person, business executive, manager, merchant
businessmen	business people, people in business
chairman	chairperson, department head, moderator, chair
Congressman	Congressional representative, member of Congress
salesmen	salespersons, salespeople, sales agents, sales representatives
workmen	workers
manmade	manufactured, handmade, hand-built
deliveryman	delivery driver, delivery clerk
housewife	homemaker

PRONOUNS

204   The use of *pronouns* is the "shorthand" of writing nouns. Once the noun has been identified, a pronoun is often used later in the sentence in place of the noun.

Luis promised *he* would come later tonight to prepare a gourmet meal.

It would be awkward to repeat the noun *Luis* again in the sentence. The pronoun *he* takes the place of the noun. The pronoun usually takes the place of a noun which has already been mentioned. The noun which gives the pronoun its meaning is called the *antecedent* (meaning "coming before").

MOHAMMED came home, took off *his* shoes, and hung up *his* coat. Dr. Michi Endo read the REPORT, put *it* in an envelope, and sent *it* to the president.

In the examples above, the antecedents are capitalized.

205   Indefinite Pronouns

Pronouns that do not refer to definite persons or things and are frequently used without antecedents are called *indefinite pronouns*. Examples are:

Singular	Plural	Singular and Plural
another, anybody, anyone, anything, each, either, every, everybody, everyone, everything, many a, neither, no one, nobody, nothing, one, somebody, someone, something	both, few, many, several, others	all, none, some

206   Personal Pronouns

Statements can be made in three ways:

● When you talk about yourself (first person)

I arrived early.
We crossed the street.

● When you talk about the person you are speaking to (second person)

Your new dress and *your* new shoes look good together.

● When you speak of anyone or anything else (third person)

His score made it impossible for *them* to win.

Pronouns having different forms to indicate person are called *personal pronouns*.

Note: Pronouns and verbs are the only parts of speech to change their form when indicating person.

	Singular	Plural
The person speaking: (first person)	I, my, mine, me	we, our, ours

This is *my* paper. *Our* play will be in the competition next month.

	Singular	*Plural*
The person spoken to: (second person)	you, your, yours,	you, your, yours

Your hair looks terrific! *You* all have a chance to get a high grade.

Some other person or thing: (third person)	he, his, him, she, her, hers, it, its,	they, their, theirs, them

Her coat is red. Pass out the plates to *them*, please.

207 Compound Pronouns

Compound pronouns are the *-self, -selves* form of the personal pronouns.

(first person)	myself	ourselves
(second person)	yourself	yourselves
(third person)	himself, herself, itself	themselves

208 Generic Pronouns

Generic pronouns are those pronouns that refer to groups of persons. When the pronouns *they* or *their* are used, the sex of group members is not indicated. Traditionally, however, the words *he, his,* or *him* have been used generically to indicate any member of a group:

Each student must bring *his* books to school every day.

This practice is now being avoided by many who feel it discriminatory to apply the masculine pronoun to a group of females or a group of males *and* females. Alternatives include:

1. Eliminating the pronoun.

   Each student must bring books to school every day.

2. Changing from singular to plural.

   All students must bring their books to school every day.

3. Using words which do not indicate gender. (*you, individual, person, one*)

   Avoid: *He* must determine *his* own special interests and dreams.

   Use: *Each person* must determine *individual* special interests and dreams.

4. Using job titles instead of the pronoun.

   Avoid: *He* should be able to sell houses effectively.

   Use: The *real estate agent* should be able to sell houses effectively.

5. Changing the pronoun to an article.

   Avoid: The doctor uses *his* patient charts to summarize treatment decisions.

   Use: The doctor uses *the* patient charts to summarize treatment decisions.

6. Changing to passive voice.

   Avoid: *He* should inform the Dean immediately of all academic concerns.

   Use: The Dean should be informed immediately of all academic concerns.

7. Adding names to eliminate generic usage.

   Avoid: The manufacturer made the announcement to *his* customers.

   Use: The manufacturer, *Mr. Bob Kowalski,* made the announcement to *his* customers.

8. Repeating the noun instead of using the pronoun.

   Avoid: If the taxpayer has a question concerning allowable deductions, *he* can call the Internal Revenue Service.

   Use: If the taxpayer has a question concerning allowable deductions, *the taxpayer* can call the Internal Revenue Service.

9. Including the feminine pronoun. *(she or he, his or her)*

   Avoid: A medical student's goal is to complete *his* medical training and begin to practice medicine.

   Use: A medical student's goal is to complete *his or her* medical training and begin to practice medicine.

Note: Alternatives 1-8 are preferred, since alternative 9 often results in awkward sentences.

209   Nominative, Objective, and Possessive Case

Just as pronouns change form to indicate person, pronouns also change form to indicate case.

The *nominative case* is used when the pronoun is the:

● *Subject* (what the sentence is about)

She (not *her*) has been elected president of the National Honor Society.

● *Complement* (completing, or adding meaning to, the verb)

It might be *he* (not *him*).

The *objective case* is used when the pronoun is the:

● *Object of the Verb*

Eduardo gave Suzanne and *me* (not *I*) help on the problem.

● *Object of a Preposition*

The briefcase was a present for *me* (not *I*).

● *Subject or Object of an Infinitive* (verb beginning with "to")

The owner asked *her* (not *she*) to apply. (*Her* is the subject of "to apply.")

Did Toby ask Lila Mae to answer *me* (not *I*)? (*Me* is the object of "to answer.")

The *possessive case* is used to indicate possession. When the possessive pronoun comes before the noun, use *her, his, its, my, our, their,* or *your.* When the possessive pronoun is separated from the noun it *modifies* (tells something about), use *hers, his, its, mine, ours, theirs,* or *yours.*

My shoes are right here. (*with* noun)

The shoes in the corner are *mine.* (*apart* from noun)

Be careful not to confuse the possessive case of pronouns with similar-sounding *contractions* (shortened words or phrases where an apostrophe indicates omitted letters or words).

Possessive Pronoun	*Contraction*
its	it's (shortened "it is")
your	you're (shortened "you are")
their	they're (shortened "they are")
theirs	there's (shortened "there is")
whose	who's (shortened "who is")

Use Table 2-1 to choose the right nominative, objective, or possessive case of the pronoun.

TABLE 2-1

Pronoun Case

Nominative	Objective	Possessive	
		With Noun	**Apart from Noun**
I, we	me, us	my, our	mine, ours
you	you	your	yours
he, she, it	him, her, it	his, her, its	his, hers, its
they	them	their	theirs
who	whom	whose	whose
that	that	that	that
whoever	whomever	whose	whose
which	which	which	which
what	what		

VERBS

210   The *subject* and *verb* are the two required parts of any sentence. While a noun or pronoun within a sentence may provide the subject doing the action or the object being acted upon, it is the *verb* that provides the action. The verb describes what the subject does or is, or what is happening to it.

Most sentence errors occur through the improper use of verbs. Therefore, an understanding of the way verbs are used within a sentence can increase your ability to communicate accurately and effectively.

211   **Role of the Verb**

Within a sentence, verbs can make statements, give commands, or ask questions.

Statements: The report is now complete.
Suzanne Richter will be the next president.

Commands: Answer the door, please.
Remain here until I return.

Questions: Who will attend the luncheon?
Is it your coat?

212   **Active/Passive Voice**

Verbs indicate whether the subject is completing the action of the sentence (*active voice*) or is being acted upon (*passive voice*).

Active Voice: Miss Levester fixed the car.
The agent mailed the pictures.

(The subjects, *Miss Levester* and *the agent*, performed the action indicated by the verb.)

Passive Voice: The roses were arranged by Ben.
Mario was promoted last week.

(The subjects, *roses* and *Mario*, received the action indicated by the verb.)

213   Subject/Verb Agreement

A verb should agree with the subject of the sentence in both *person* and *number*. A singular subject (one) requires a singular verb. A plural subject (more than one) requires a plural form of the verb.

Singular Subject/
   Singular Verb: The report *is* (not *are*) almost complete.
                      She *is* (not *are*) the new electrician.

Plural Subject/
   Plural Verb: Three women *were* (not *was*) ice skating.
                      The men *were* (not *was*) taking gourmet cooking.

A *compound subject* requires a plural verb.

Compound Subject/
   Plural Verb: Bill and Mary *were* (not *was*) tied for second place.

Collective nouns take singular verbs when the group acts together and plural verbs when the members of the group act individually.

Group Acting Together: The committee *recommends* a complete reorganization.

Members Acting
   Independently: The staff *are* at their desks.

214   Helping Verbs

Helping (auxiliary) verbs are joined to other verbs to indicate voice or tense. The following are commonly used helping verbs:

are	have been	shall be
can	is	shall have
can be	may	shall have been
can have	may be	should
could	may have	should be
could be	may have been	should have
could have	might	should have been
could have been	might be	will
do	might have	will be
did	might have been	will have
had	must	will have been
had been	must be	would
has	must have	would be
has been	must have been	would have
have	shall	would have been

215   **Verb Tense**

   The tense of a verb indicates the time of an event. There are six tenses of verbs: past, past perfect, present, present perfect, future, and future perfect. Table 2-2 will provide quick reference for the use of the six verb tenses.

216   **Past Participle**

   With regular verbs, the past participle verb form is exactly the same as the past verb form—"d" or "ed" is simply added to the base verb form. With irregular verbs, however, the past participle form is often different from the past verb form. It is always the past participle verb form that is used to form perfect tenses.

217   **Regular and Irregular Verbs**

   For all regular verbs, verb tenses are formed as indicated in Table 2-2. Irregular verbs vary in form and do not follow normal patterns for present, past, future, and past participle verb forms. The dictionary always indicates the principal parts of all irregular verbs. If the principle parts are not shown, the verb is regular in form. Below is a list of some of the most common irregular verbs.

IRREGULAR VERBS

Present	Past	Past Participle	Present	Past	Past Participle
am, are, is*	was, were	been	grow	grew	grown
become	became	become	know	knew	known
begin	began	begun	leave	left	left
bring	brought	brought	lie	lay	lain (to rest)
buy	bought	bought	lay	laid	laid (to place)
come	came	come	make	made	made
do	did	done	pay	paid	paid
drive	drove	driven	run	ran	run
fall	fell	fallen	see	saw	seen
get	got	got	set	set	set
give	gave	given	spring	sprang	sprung
go	went	gone	take	took	taken
			write	wrote	written

*form of "to be"

ADJECTIVES

218   *Adjectives* are words which provide additional information about nouns and pronouns. They tell such things as which one, how many, and what kind.

TABLE 2-2

Verb Tense

	Past	Past Perfect	Present	Present Perfect	Future	Future Perfect
Time	started and completed in past	started and completed in past before some other past action	now	action started in past, continuing in present	will happen in future	will be completed in future
Form	regular verbs* add "d" or "ed" to base form	had + past participle	base form (third person singular adds "s")	have or has + past participle	shall or will + base form	shall or will + have + past participle
Examples	I ordered you ordered he/she/it ordered	I had ordered you had ordered he/she/it had ordered	I order you order he/she/it orders	I have ordered you have ordered he/she/it has ordered	I shall order you will order he/she/it will order	I shall have ordered you will have ordered he/she/it will have ordered
	we ordered you ordered they ordered	we had ordered you had ordered they had ordered	we order you order they order	we have ordered you have ordered they have ordered	we shall order you will order they will order	we shall have ordered you will have ordered they will have ordered

Note: For irregular verbs, consult your dictionary for past and past participle verb forms.

Descriptive adjectives describe a noun or pronoun.

The *little* spot on my *red* blouse was overlooked.
Thirteen girls arrived at the *square* building in the middle of the
Calle Ocho Festival.

Definite (the) and indefinite (a, an) adjectives are referred to
as *articles*. Definite articles refer to a specific person or thing;
indefinite articles refer to any person or thing. In using the indefinite article, use "an" before words that begin with a vowel (*a, e, i,
o,* and short *u*) and also with words that sound like they begin with
a vowel (*hour*). For all words beginning with a consonant (except
for those that sound like they begin with a vowel), use the indefinite article "a."

Definite: *The* girl came to *the* early show.

Indefinite: *An* individual must study hard in order to pass this course.
                   A chain is only as strong as its weakest link.

Pronouns can be used as adjectives when they modify nouns
within a sentence.

Her grade on the test was higher than *his* grade.
Their grandmother and *our* grandfather once were dating.
This paper has many examples of *those* errors.

ADVERBS

219   *Adverbs* are words that modify verbs, adjectives, or
other adverbs. They provide additional information by answering
the questions "when," "where," "how," or "how much."

when: Enrique *now* knows the entire story.
                  Your order will be ready *soon*.

where: The backgammon tournament will be held *there*.
                  We found it *there* in your seat.

how: Run *quickly* to the store before it closes.
                  She *carefully* rewired the electrical connection.

how much: They complained *repeatedly*.

220   Comparisons with Adjectives/Adverbs

Adjectives and adverbs can be used to compare one person or
thing with other persons or things. When there is a comparison
between two persons or things, the *comparative degree* is used.
The *superlative degree* is used when comparisons are made between three or more persons or things. Table 2-3 provides a quick
reference for using adjectives and adverbs in comparisons.

TABLE 2-3

Comparisons with Adjectives/Adverbs

	Base Form	Comparative Degree (comparing two persons or things)	Superlative Degree (comparing three or more persons or things)
One Syllable Words	old nice	add "er" to base form* older nicer	add "est" to base form* oldest nicest
Two Syllable Words	happy	add "er" to base form* or use *more* or *less* before base form happier more happy less happy	add "est" to base form* or use *most* or *least* before base form happiest most happy least happy
Words of More Than Two Syllables	intelligent	add *more* or *less* before base form more intelligent less intelligent	add *most* or *least* before base form most intelligent least intelligent

* Note: There are some minor spelling changes in some words.

Note: A few one-syllable words are written with *more* or *less* added to the base form in the comparative degree and *most* or *least* added to the base form in the superlative degree.

221   Troublesome Adjectives/Adverbs/Nouns

There are some words that can function as either adjectives or adverbs and are often confused. In addition, some adjectives and adverbs are confused with similar-sounding nouns and verbs. The following is a list of some of these confusing combinations.

Adapt/Adept/Adopt: The firm will *adapt* this form to fit the purchasing department's new requirements. (adjust)
Mary and Leonard were both very *adept* at learning shorthand. (skilled)
Jim and Barbara Gray will *adopt* a son. (choose)

Affect/Effect: The heat *affected* our appetites. (influenced—verb)
The committee *effected* a compromise. (accomplished or produced—verb)
The heat had an adverse *effect* on our appetites. (result—noun)

All Ready/Already: We are *all ready* to go now. (completely prepared)
Have they left *already*? (before an understood time)

All Right/Alright: We were relieved to hear that they were *all right*. (satisfactory)
Alright—a nonstandard form of *all right*. *Alright* is not considered grammatically acceptable.

Allowed/Aloud: Children are not *allowed* to attend. (permitted)
Pam read the poem *aloud* to her students. (out loud)

Any One/Anyone: *Any one* of these courses will satisfy the requirement. (any person or thing of one group)
Has *anyone* seen my purse? (anybody)

Bad/Badly: My car is *badly* in need of repair. (*badly* meaning very much)
It looks *bad* for our team. (After *look, smell, sound*, etc., *bad* is preferred.)

Beside/Besides: She sat *beside* me during the entire play. (next to)
Besides my television, the thieves took the stereo and video recorder. (in addition, also)

Between/Among: The choice is *between* Bart and Ricardo. (*Between* is used when *two* persons or things are objects or with terms such as *treaty, agreement,* or *discussion*.)
They always enjoy being *among* celebrities. (*Among* is used when *three or more* persons or things are objects and no close relationship is indicated.)

Capital/Capitol: The *capital* of Colorado is Denver. (*Capital* is used to mean a seat of government; a term in finance, accounting, and architecture; chief and first rate; capital letter; and capital punishment.)

The signing of the bill will take place in the *Capitol* Building at noon. (*Capitol* is used to mean the buildings used by Congress and state legislatures.)

Every One/Everyone: *Every one* of them had a choice. (each one)

Will *everyone* be coming to the party? (everybody)

Farther/Further: Your house is *farther* than I thought. (actual distance)

His statement could not be *further* from the truth. (additional; greater distance [in time or quantity])

Fewer/Less: Our debts were *fewer* in those days. (We had 10 debts then; we have 21 now.)

Our debts were *less* in those days. (We owed $2100 then; we owe $4800 now.)

Foreword/Forward: In the *foreword* of the book, the author mentions her years of research. (preface)

Come *forward* a little into the light so I can see your new dress. (toward the front, progressive)

Formally/Formerly: He was *formally* accepted as a member after the initiation. (in a formal manner)

She was *formerly* the Ambassador to Britain. (previously, before)

Forth/Fourth: From that day *forth*, she was never the same. (forward, onward in time)

It was the *fourth* time I tried to contact the drama department. (after third)

Good/Well: The chili smells *good*. (adjective only)

Ann is *well* enough to join Karen at the game. (adjective or adverb)

Knew/New: She *knew* Dr. Ortiz before taking her class. (acquainted with)

We filled our house with *new* furniture. (fresh, unused)

Last/Latest: Bennie Moore was the *last* one to arrive for the Academic Council meeting. (final)

This is the *latest* announcement. (most recent)

Later/Latter: Enjoy yourself, it's *later* than you think. (after the usual or proper time)

Karen Paiva and Jan Gordillo were the two contestants; the *latter* was the winner. (second of two)

Least/Leased: Arriving on time was the *least* of our worries today. (smallest)

Maxine *leased* a condominium near the Omni Hotel. (rented)

Liable/Libel: The club is *liable* for any damages on the rented room. (responsible)

The author was sued for *libel* after the book was published. (injury through written or printed statements)

Loose/Lose: My earring was *loose*, and I lost it. (not secure)

The team did not want to *lose* the match. (suffer a loss)

May Be/Maybe: My picture *may be* in the next CETA READER. (verb)

Maybe we should call, if they don't arrive soon. (adverb)

Passed/Past: To my surprise, I *passed* the algebra test. (verb)

In *past* events, the rules have been different. (noun, adjective, adverb, preposition)

Personal/Personnel: My decision to leave was a very *personal* one. (private)

The *personnel* at your organization seem very enthusiastic. (the employees)

Principal/Principle: Mr. John Kushner was the very popular *principal* of the school. (chief official, capital sum of money)

It wasn't the decision that was made, rather it was the *principle* of the thing that was important to Mary. (basic truth)

Real/Really: Maxine Kamin was a *real* friend. (true, actual—adjective)

Are you *really* going to vote for the amendment? (actually—adverb)

Some/Sum: *Some* of the audience began to leave. (part)

What is the *sum* of all your expenses? (total)

Some Time/ Sometime/ Sometimes: It was *some time* before the farmer returned from the market. (a period of time)

Sometime later this week, we will schedule a conference call. (at an unspecified time)

Sometimes it is hard to understand written reports. (now and then)

Stationary/Stationery: The table remained *stationary* on the stage. (fixed)

Most business offices use letterhead *stationery* in their correspondence. (writing paper)

Sure/Surely:

I am *sure* you can learn this job. (adjective)
Surely you don't want to quit now? (adverb)

Than/Then:

Social security rates are higher *than* they were when I first started to work. (comparison)
Wait until the car stops; *then* you can get out safely. (at that time)

Their/There:

Their interest was in the individualized instruction. (pronoun)
Put it *there* on the table. (in that place—adverb)

To/Too/Two:

Come *to* the store with me. (preposition)
Ricky wants to come, *too*. (also—adverb)
Two teachers were assigned to the same class. (number following one—adjective or noun)

Weak/Week:

He was too *weak* to climb any further. (not strong)
This *week* we have a vacation from school to celebrate the holidays. (seven successive days)

Weather/Whether:

The *weather* remained sunny during our entire vacation. (state of the atmosphere—noun)
Whether or not we vote, our issue still cannot win. (regardless—conjunction)

CONJUNCTIONS

222   *Conjunctions* are words used to connect two words, phrases, or clauses. *Coordinating conjunctions* connect words, phrases, or clauses that are alike. The most common coordinating conjunctions are *and, but, for, or, nor,* and *yet*.

Dr. Eduardo Padron *and* Dr. Castell Bryant were honored at the banquet.
The secretaries like their jobs, *but* they want to continue their educations.

Correlative conjunctions are *pairs* of words that connect two like words, phrases, or clauses. The most common pairs include:

both/and   either/or   neither/nor   not/but
not only/but also   whether/or

Either Dr. Vicente *or* his assistant will perform the surgery in the morning.
Neither Lourdes *nor* I remembered the appointment yesterday.
Both Russell *and* I are looking forward to seeing you tomorrow.

PREPOSITIONS

223   A *preposition* is a word which connects a noun or pronoun to another word in the sentence and shows the relationship between the two words.

> The man walked *between* the trees.

In this sentence, the preposition *between* shows the relationship between the man and the trees.

Ὰ The phrase formed by connecting the preposition to the noun or pronoun serving as the *object of the preposition* is called a *prepositional phrase.*

> Yolanda placed a call *to her editor.*
> Greg searched high and low *for the file.*
> Please give it *to me.*

Note: Pronouns following a preposition must be in the objective case (see ¶ 209).

Commonly Used Prepositions

about	above	across	after	against
among	around	at	before	behind
below	beside	between	by	down
during	except	for	from	in
into	like	of	off	on
over	past	round	since	through
till	to	under	until	up
upon	with	within	without	

INTERJECTIONS

224   An *interjection* is a word expressing strong emotion, usually followed by an exclamation mark. The word may be written alone, or it may be used within a sentence. Common interjections include:

> Hooray!   Great!   Oh!   Terrific!   Wonderful!

FREQUENT GRAMMATICAL ERRORS

225   Common grammatical errors are shown in the following paragraphs. To avoid making similar errors yourself, study the incorrect examples, the rules involved, and the corrected examples.

226   Subject/Verb Agreement

Incorrect:	The girl hop across the puddle.
RULE:	Singular subject takes singular verb.
Correct:	The girl *hops* across the puddle.

Incorrect:	The boys arranges to have transportation to the game.
RULE:	Plural subject takes plural verb.
Correct:	The boys *arrange* to have transportation to the game.

Incorrect:	I is going on vacation.
RULE:	First-person subject takes first-person verb.
Correct:	I *am* going on vacation.

227   Ambiguous Modifiers

Incorrect:	Loudly protesting, the wallet was taken from the man. Bob said he loved her always. Hissing and snarling, the woman was attacked by a lion. I caught a dolphin standing on the front of the boat.
RULE:	Modifying words or phrases should be placed as close as possible to the words or phrases they modify.
Correct:	*Loudly protesting*, the man had his wallet taken. Bob said he *always loved* her. The woman was attacked by a *hissing and snarling lion*. *While standing on the front of the boat*, I caught a dolphin.

228   Parallel Construction

Incorrect:	Sally's grades are better than Russell. Dr. Padron attended a meeting in the morning, performing surgery at noon, and enjoyed the ballet in the evening. Karen Paiva plays her guitar and singing. The dollar is worth less than some countries. Stephen is more interested in archery than his friends. We waited in the rain, and I finally see the President.
RULE:	Parallel construction requires balancing of the grammatical structure. Compare like nouns and avoid shifts in tense.
Correct:	Sally's grades are better than *Russell's grades*. Dr. Padron attended a meeting in the morning, *performed* surgery at noon, and enjoyed the ballet in the evening.

Karen Paiva plays her guitar and *sings*.
The dollar is worth less than some *countries' currencies*.
Stephen is more interested in archery than his *friends are*.
We waited in the rain, and I finally *saw* the President.

229   Sentence Fragments

Incorrect: Who turned out to be my best friend.
                     If you want to be a successful writer.
                     To make this day a huge success.

RULE: To be correct, a sentence must contain a subject and a verb and must express a complete thought.

Correct: It was Ricky Gettings who turned out to be my best friend.
                     If you want to be a successful writer, you must practice writing something every day.
                     To make this day a huge success, the committee planned carefully for the picnic.

230   Run-On Sentences

Incorrect: No one wanted to help us, they were afraid of losing their places in line.
                     One problem the team had was inexperience, the other one was a lack of leadership.
                     I really like football I support the Miami Dolphins.

RULE: When two independent clauses are closely related, they can be separated by a semicolon. When there is no close relationship, punctuate the independent clauses as separate sentences.

Correct: No one wanted to help us. They were afraid of losing their places in line. (no close relationship)
                     One problem the team had was inexperience; the other one was a lack of leadership. (closely related)
                     I really like football; I support the Miami Dolphins. (closely related)

231   Words Ending in "One" or "Body"

Incorrect: One of us require first aid.
                     Nobody want to attend class today.
                     Everyone need to visit an advisor.

RULE: Words ending in "one" or "body" require a singular verb.

Correct: One of us *requires* first aid.
                     Nobody *wants* to attend class today.
                     Everyone *needs* to visit an advisor.

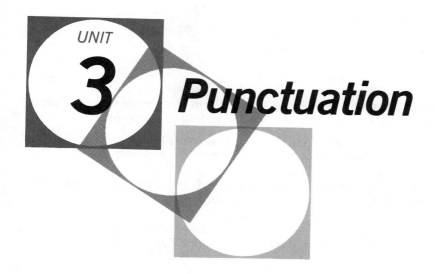

UNIT 3 *Punctuation*

3

AMPERSAND

301   The ampersand may be used freely in tables, bills, technical material, etc.—but should not be used generally.

Their business is located at Spring *and* Elm Streets.

In business names. Some business names incorporate the ampersand.

She is a partner in Morales & O'Leary.

APOSTROPHE

302   The apostrophe is used to create possessive forms of certain nouns. The apostrophe indicates four major relationships

- **Owning:**   the depositors' money.
                    the library's book.

- **Having:**   the soldier's rifle.
                    the student's library book.

- **Originating:** the author's book.
                    the artist's painting.

33

- **Measuring:** a dollar's worth.
  an hour's drive.
  a stone's throw.

Nouns not ending in an s or z sound. Form the possessive of a noun *not ending in an s or z sound* by adding *apostrophe s*.

Roberta's account	a teacher's book
Lou's concrete	the church's steeple

Singular nouns ending in an s or z sound. Form the possessive of a singular noun *ending in an s or z sound*:

One-Syllable Noun *(add 's)*	*Noun of More Than* *One Syllable* *(add ')*
Sue Morse's cow	Leon Contreras' book

Note: Some writers make this decision on the basis of the difficulty of pronunciation rather than the number of syllables.

Difficult to Pronounce *if a Syllable Were Added* *(add ')*	*Not Difficult to Pronounce* *with an Additional Syllable* *(add 's, which adds the* *additional syllable ezz)*
Ulysses' coat	the Adams's home
the Knights of Pythias' hall	Amalgamated Service's store

Plural nouns ending in an s or z sound. Form the possessive of a plural noun ending in an *s* or *z* sound by adding an apostrophe.

both Henrys' surnames	three accountants' offices
two clubs' meetings	four officers' ledgers
pair of stars' light	five hours' work
ten dollars' worth	three hours' drive

Other types of nouns. Generally, it is better not to use the possessive form with *nouns other than those representing people, animals, organizations, geographic locations, time, value, distance, and celestial bodies.* Instead, use one of these forms:

- a phrase incorporating words such as *of, in, by, for,* etc.

    the transistors (*of, in, for*) the TV

- the noun as a modifier.

    the television transistors

Expressions suggesting personification, however, may be stated in the possessive form.

    virtue's reward

Note: Some writers use the apostrophe to create possessive forms of nouns other than those representing people, animals, organizations, geographic locations, etc.

303   Possessive Forms of Pronouns

Special possessive forms. Personal pronouns and the relative pronoun *who* have special possessive forms. The apostrophe is not used to create their possessive forms.

Pronoun	Possessive	Pronoun	Possessive
I	my, mine	we	our, ours
you	your, yours	they	their, theirs
she	her, hers	it	its
he	his, his	who	whose

Note: Do not confuse the possessive forms of pronouns (*its, whose,* etc.) with contractions (*it's, who's,* etc.).

Possessive Forms	*Contractions*
its value	it's time to go (it is)
whose idea	who's ready? (who is)

Indefinite pronouns. Some indefinite pronouns have regular possessive forms requiring the use of *apostrophe s* .

Indefinite Pronoun	*Possessive Form*
one	one's business
everybody	everybody's sunset
another	another's virtue
someone else	someone else's problem

Other indefinite pronouns have no *regular* possessive form; use an *of* phrase to create the possessive form.

each . . . . . of each	all . . . . of all	many . . . . . of many
several . . . of several	few . . . . . . of few,	
	of a few	

304   Possessive Forms of Abbreviations and Names

Singular and plural. *Singular* possessives of abbreviations are formed by adding *apostrophe s* to the abbreviation.

SPCA	the SPCA's animal shelter
C.P.S.	the C.P.S.'s certificate
M.D.	the M.D.'s office

Plural possessives are formed by adding *an apostrophe* to the plural form of the abbreviation.

SPCAs	three local SPCAs' shelters
C.P.S.s	both the C.P.S.s' certificates
M.D.s	two M.D.s' practices

Personal and organizational names. Possessive forms of personal and organizational names ending with abbreviations or numbers follow the general rule:

Singular *Add Apostrophe s*	*Plural* *Add an Apostrophe* *to the Plural Form*
Donald Dadey, Jr.'s bank	three local AAAs' offices
Henry Winthrop, III's driveway	
the AAA's office	

Note: Current trends favor eliminating some punctuation in personal and organizational names. The preferences of the person or organization should prevail in these cases:

- The comma before a surname prefix may be omitted.

    Donald Dadey Jr.   Henry Winthrop III

- The apostrophe indicating possession in an organizational name may be omitted.

    Writer's Digest ...... but .....*Ladies Home Journal*
    Captain A's Place .... but ..... Mister Ds Pub

305   Where to Apply the Indicators of Possession

Joint or common possession. *Joint* or *common possession* exists when there are two or more possessors.

- If all possessors are identified by name, apply the indicator(s) of possession to the final name.

    Eva and Marie's car

- If one or more possessors are identified by a pronoun, use the possessive form of each name or pronoun identifying a possessor.

    Sharon's and his apartment
    her and Yolanda's work shift

Separate possession. *Separate possession* is indicated by applying the indicator(s) of possession to *each* noun or pronoun identifying a possessor.

    Marvin's and Janet's houses
    Mary's and Joe's bicycles

Appositives. An *appositive* is a noun used after another noun to identify or explain the first noun.

    Albert, *the waiter*

Apply the indicator(s) of possession to the final word or word element of the appositive.

    Albert, the waiter's, station

Note: An appositive may consist of a noun substitute: gerund phrase, infinitive phrase, noun clause, etc. These forms are usually avoided because of their awkwardness.

Awkward: the actor, *the tallest one's*, part in the show
Better: the tallest actor's part in the show

Awkward: the actor, *the one now talking's*, vocabulary
Better: the vocabulary of the actor now talking

Compound nouns. A *compound noun* consists of two or more words combined or used together to serve as a single noun. Apply the indicator(s) of possession to the final word or word element.

    mother+in+law   mother-in-law's
    drop+out   dropout's
    night+owl   night owl's

Note: There are no rigid patterns applicable to writing compounds solid (bookkeeper), hyphenating them (great-grandfather), or writing the words separately (jumper cable). When in doubt, consult a dictionary. Use words that *seem* like compounds, but do not appear as compounds in the dictionary, as separate words.

Gerunds. Apply the indicator(s) of possession to the noun or pronoun modifying a *gerund* (the *ing* form of a verb).

    Jacob's talking annoyed them.
    Olivia's writing was excellent.
    The Morrises' jogging kept them in shape.

Understood nouns. Apply the indicators of possession to the noun or pronoun modifying an *understood* (omitted) noun.

    Take it to the plumber's. (shop)
    Take them to the plumbers'. (shops)
    Stop at the Taylors'. (home)

Possessives modifying possessives. Avoid possessives modifying possessives by rewording.

Not: Maria's sister's camera
But: a camera belonging to Maria's sister

Not: Frank's children's toys
But: toys belonging to Frank's children

Omitted characters. When the apostrophe is used to replace omitted characters, it is placed at the exact point of the omission.

- Contractions.

would n(o)t	wouldn't (not would'nt)
did n(o)t	didn't (not did'nt)
does n(o)t	doesn't (not does'nt)
of the clock	o'clock

- Numbers.

the '37 flood   '55 was a good year

Contractions and possessives. Do not confuse pronoun contractions and possessive pronouns. (See ¶209.)

Pronoun Contractions	*Possessive Pronouns*
it's (it is, it has)	its (belonging to it)
they're (they are)	their (belonging to them)
who's (who is)	whose (belonging to whom)
you're (you are)	your (belonging to you)

306   Other Uses of Apostrophes

As a symbol. In tables, bills, technical writing, and other work in which the frequent use of abbreviations is appropriate, the apostrophe is used as a symbol.

21 feet, 7 inches: 21' 7"   5 minutes, 22 seconds: 5' 22"

As a single quotation mark. Use the apostrophe as a single quotation mark.

Peggy said, "The quotation begins, 'In the early days. . .'."

Note: If another level is needed, use regular quotation marks again.

Willie said, "Peggy said, 'The quotation begins, "In the early days. . .".'"

Plural of symbols. The apostrophe *may* be used in forming the plural of symbols.

@'s   #'s   %'s   *'s
Use @'s instead of *at*'s.

Note: Also acceptable: @s   #s $s   %s   *s

Plural of numbers. The apostrophe *may* be used to form the plural of numbers.

2's   5's   27's   100's
Do not make your *2* 's so that they look like *5* 's.

Note: Also acceptable: 2s   5s   27s   100s

Plural of letters. The apostrophe is used to form the plural of lower-case letters.

We need two *l*'s and three *k*'s to complete the sign.

Note: The apostrophe is *necessary* in this case.

The apostrophe *may* be used to form the plural of capital letters.

We need two *L*'s and three *K*'s to complete the sign.

Note: The preferable plural form of capital letters does not require an apostrophe.

We need two *L*s and three *K*s to complete the sign.

Plural of words used as words. Words used as words rather than for their meanings may be identified with apostrophes when their plural forms are used.

Paint the *and*'s and *but*'s and the sign will be completed.

307   Typewriter Spacing with the Apostrophe

	Before	After
• Ending a word, abbreviation, etc., within a sentence	0	1
• Other apostrophes	0	0

308   The Apostrophe with Other Punctuation

The apostrophe is treated as part of the word; no punctuation separates it from other parts (letters) of the word.

The pool is the Winters'. It is a large . . .
The house is the Riveras', but it . . .
The book is the managers'; they will expect . . .

ASTERISK

309   **Footnotes.** The asterisk indicates that a footnote will be found below. The asterisk is inserted immediately after the sentence, clause, phrase, word, etc., to which the footnote refers.* A pair of asterisks, typed with no intervening space, identifies the second footnote on the page.** A set of three asterisks, typed with no intervening spaces,*** identifies the third footnote on the page.

* The asterisk *follows* any other punctuation with which it appears.

** Insertion of the asterisk does not alter the conventions for spacing:
 * Leave two spaces after the end of a sentence.*_ _ If the sentence ends with a question mark or exclamation mark, spacing is the same—two spaces following the asterisk.
 * Leave one space between*_ words.
 * Following a comma,*_ leave one space after the asterisk.

*** If more than three footnotes appear on a page, most writers use numbered footnotes. See ¶ 1112.

Paragraph omission. Groups of three horizontally centered asterisks, with one space between the first and second asterisks and another between the second and third asterisks, are used to indicate the omission of one or more paragraphs.

* * *

In this example, the asterisks indicate that paragraphed material was omitted between the word *paragraphs* (the final word in the paragraph above) and the word *In* (the first word in this paragraph).

Unprintable words. Asterisks are used to indicate the omission of unprintable words. A group of three asterisks without intervening spaces may be substituted for each unprintable word, or each letter in the unprintable word may be represented by an asterisk.

He was called a *** and a ***.
She was called a *****.

310   Typewriter Spacing with the Asterisk

	Before	After
Following a word, abbreviation, etc., in a sentence.	0	1
At the end of a sentence.	0	2
In a footnote. See ¶ 309 for one acceptable style.	0-5	0
Substituted for an unprintable word within a sentence.	1	1
Substituted for an unprintable word at the end of a sentence.	1	0

BRACE

311   The brace is used to join related material, most frequently in law documents, tables, and display work—such as advertising. In typewritten material, the brace is frequently made with two or more parentheses. It can be drawn freehand or with a plastic template.

Law Document,
Parentheses: as to _____

Law Document,
Freehand: as to _____

Advertisement, Drawn with a Plastic Template: Lots $\begin{Bmatrix} 384 \\ 986 \\ 217 \end{Bmatrix}$ $3.88

BRACKETS

312   Brackets are used to identify *inserted* material:

- Clarification or corrections in material written by others.

    "Tell them [the movers] to load it."
    "It was a heart-wrenching [sic] scene."

Note: The word *sic* in brackets means *thus* or *so*. It tells the reader that, even though there is something unusual—possibly incorrect— about the immediately preceding part of the quotation, it is repro- duced exactly (*thus* or *so*) as it appeared in the original.

- Notes on pronunciation.

    Esau [(H)e′ saw]

- Parenthetical expression within another parenthetical expres- sion.

    (It should be noted that all the young people [through age 20] were invited.)

Making brackets. Since most typewriter keyboards do not include brackets, they are usually:

Typed Using Diagonals and Underscores	*Drawn Freehand or with a Ruler*	*Drawn with a Plastic Template*
⌐sic⌐	[sic]	[sic]

313   Typewriter Spacing with Brackets

Opening Bracket:

	Before	*After*
• Within a sentence.	1	0
• Immediately preceding a separate sentence.	2	0
• Immediately preceding another punctuation mark.	1	0

Closing Bracket:

• Following parenthetical matter within a sentence.	0	1
• Following normal end-of-sentence punctuation.	0	2
• Followed by another punctuation mark.	0	0

Note: For placement of brackets relative to other punctuation, see ¶ 342. Conventions prescribed for parentheses apply also to brackets replacing parentheses.

COLON

314   The colon identifies a relationship in which an *introductory expression* (preceding the colon) introduces an *explanatory* or *illustrative expression* (following the colon).

Introduction: explanation or illustration.

Introductory expressions. An *introductory expression* preceding a colon:

• Should have a subject and predicate.

These plants are found locally: magnolia, pine, and azalea.

• Should cause the reader to *anticipate* the explanation or illustration that will follow the colon.

There are three reasons for that course of action: it is right; it is prudent; it is profitable.

Note: Expressions indicating anticipation are *such as, as follows, including,* etc.

Please proceed *as follows* : thread the needle before you turn the machine on.

- May *imply*—rather than state—that something will follow.

The reason was important: it was raining.

- Should be near the colon. Intervening words should not distract the reader from the relationship identified by the colon.

Not: The Federal Reserve will mandate an important change, best understood by economists and bankers, but important to others who have a stake in the economy as well: an adjustment to the discount rate.

But: The Federal Reserve will mandate an important change: an adjustment to the discount rate. That action is best understood by economists and bankers but is important to all who have a stake in the economy.

- Should not end with a verb or preposition.

Not: The box contains: pens, erasers, paper, ink, etc.
But: The box contains pens, erasers, paper, ink, etc.

Not: The mix consists of: cement, sand, lime, and water.
But: The mix consists of cement, sand, lime, and water.
Unless: The listed items appear on separate lines.

The box contains:	The mix consists of:
Pens	Cement
Erasers	Sand
Paper	Lime
Ink, etc.	Water

Explanatory or illustrative expressions. The *explanatory or illustrative expression* following the colon may consist of:

- One or more sentences.

There were several good reasons not to go: The show was dull. The weather was bad. Several people were ill.

- A clause or clauses.

We were reluctant to go: the show was sure to be dull.

- A word or words.

One important aspect of the show made us reluctant to go: dullness.

- Items on a list.

  Please load the following furniture:
     1 Desk
     2 Chairs
     1 Couch
     3 Tables

- A quotation.

  O. Henry wrote: "A straw vote only shows which way the hot air blows."

Capitalization with the colon. Capitalize after a colon:

- The first letter of each proper noun and proper adjective—and the pronoun I.

  This is the reason: Henry would not go.

- When the colon is followed immediately by a quoted sentence.

  The guard said: "You cannot go that way."

- If the expression *after the colon* is a complete sentence *that is the dominant or more general element*.

  Here is the reason: Atmospheric pressure at sea level is not always the same. (The element following the colon is a complete sentence. It is the dominant element.)

  Atmospheric pressure at sea level is not always the same: that is reason enough. (The element following the colon is a complete sentence, but it is not dominant. Do not capitalize after the colon.)

  Here is the reason: atmospheric pressure at sea level. (The element following the colon is dominant, but it is not a complete sentence. Do not capitalize after the colon.)

- If two or more statements follow the colon.

  Three people will be involved: The first will drive the vehicle. The second will navigate. The third will observe.

- Each item on a line-by-line list.

  These were the items of greatest value:
     Automobile
     Vase
     Painting

Note: Item numbers in an enumeration, quantities on a list, or both, do not alter the rule: Capitalize each item on a line-by-line list.

1. Automobile	2 Automobiles	1. 2 Automobiles
2. Vase	5 Vases	2. 5 Vases
3. Painting	3 Paintings	3. 3 Paintings

Literary references. The colon is used in literary references to:

• Separate title and subtitle.

    Spelling: A Mnemonics Approach

• Separate volume number and page number in footnotes and bibliographies.

    Volume 21, pages 61 and 62.   21:61-62.

• Separate city of publication and name of publisher in footnotes and bibliographies.

    Ann Arbor: University of Michigan Press.

Note: See ¶¶ 1110-1115 for footnote and bibliography styles.

Biblical references. Biblical references are frequently written with a colon.

    Genesis 2:5 refers to Chapter 2, Verse 5 of the Book of Genesis.

Ratios and proportions. A colon may be used to express a ratio or proportion.

    The axle has a ratio of 3.5:1. Or
    The axle has a ratio of 3.5 to 1. Or
    The axle has a ratio of 3.5-to-1.

Other uses. Other uses for the colon:

• The salutation of a business letter may be

    Followed by a colon. See ¶ 1008.
    Followed by no punctuation. See ¶ 1008.

Note: The salutation of a personal letter is usually followed by a comma.

• A colon may be used between sets of initials identifying those responsible for a business letter. See ¶ 1014.

    MAB:LER   MAB:ler   mab:ler

• A colon separates hours and minutes in the statement of times of day.

    3:00 p.m.   It happened between 5:30 a.m. and 6:45 p.m.

315   **Typewriter Spacing with the Colon**

	Before	After
• In normal use within a sentence.	0	2
• Time of day, reference initials, ratios.	0	0

316   **The Colon with Other Punctuation**

- Dash, ¶¶ 326, 328.
- Parentheses, ¶ 342.
- Quotation marks, ¶¶ 355, 356, 364.

COMMA

317   **Following the Introductory Element of a Sentence**

The introductory element of a sentence

- Is found at the beginning of the sentence.
- Precedes the subject and verb of the main clause.
- May consist of one or more words, a phrase, or a clause.

> *Wait*, and your turn will come.
> *Remembering the snow*, they dressed warmly.
> *If the smaller rock is heavier*, it is more dense.

A comma is frequently used after an introductory element. Some writers use a comma after the introductory element most of the time. Most writers use a comma after the introductory element only if:

- The clarity of the sentence is improved.
- The sentence becomes easier to read—silently or aloud.
- It is desirable (for effect) to create or lengthen a pause.

A comma after the introductory element is *likely* to improve the sentence if the introductory element:

- Introduces a question.

> The question is, will they go?

- Introduces a quotation.

> The operator asked, "Did you complete the call?"

- Is a dependent clause.

> When the light goes on, we shall see.
> If the bank calls, take a message.

- Is a request or command.

> Remember, the meeting is at 3:00 p.m.

- Is a mild interjection.

> Oh, it always rains when we plan a picnic.

- Is *transitional*, providing a transition in meaning from the previous sentence.

> On the other hand, a ring may not be the proper gift.
> Well, water was not the answer.
> Therefore, we shall try again.

- Is an independent comment on the thought expressed by the sentence.

> In my opinion, the accused is guilty.
> Obviously, they did not anticipate the problem.
> As I see it, we can expect a change.

- Is an infinitive, participial, or prepositional phrase.

> *To run*, wild horses will forego other pleasures.
> *Running wild*, horses soon tire.
> *In the wild*, horses obey the herding instinct.

Most writers omit the comma after:

- A short introductory phrase if the clarity of the sentence does not suffer.

> *At the office* they discussed the proposal.

- An introductory adverb.

> *Suddenly* the deal was called off.

318 Following an Introductory Element Within a Sentence

Any of the elements used to introduce sentences (¶ 317) may be used to introduce a clause within a sentence. An introductory element *within a sentence* should be followed by a comma *if* the comma adds to the clarity or readability of the sentence.

> The veterinarian explained that *to run*, wild horses will forego other pleasures.

Note: The internal introductory infinitive phrase *to run* is not preceded by a comma because it *introduces* the main clause, *wild horses will forego other pleasures*. It does not *interrupt* the sentence. The conventions for using commas after internal introductory elements are the same as those for elements introducing sentences. See ¶ 317.

319 Setting Off Interrupting Words, Phrases, and Clauses

A *nonessential* word, phrase, or clause within a sentence is set off by commas.

- A *nonessential element* is not essential to the meaning or structure of the sentence; an *essential element* is necessary to the meaning or structure of the sentence.

- An essential element identifies or designates that which it modifies. While a nonessential element may supply supplementary information, it is information beyond that necessary for identification.

- A nonessential element can be identified by reading the sentence aloud. If, in a proper reading, the voice *falls* when the inserted element is read, the inserted element is *nonessential*. If the voice *rises*, the inserted element is *essential*.

- A nonessential element interrupts the flow of the sentence from subject to verb to object or complement.

320   Examples of Interrupting Elements

Words.

> It is, *nevertheless*, a good idea.
> It seems, *therefore*, that the idea has merit.

Note: As used above, *nevertheless* and *therefore* interrupt the flow of the sentence, are nonessential elements of the sentence, and can be identified by the tendency of the voice to fall when they are read. Contrast these uses with their use as essential elements (no commas) in the following sentences:

> Do not use the word *nevertheless* too often.
> Did the student spell *therefore* correctly?

Phrases.

- *Infinitive*

  Nonessential: The place, *to be blunt*, is a mess.
  Essential: The place *to be blunt* is at the meeting.

- *Participial*

  Nonessential: The executives, *planning to attend the conference*, made airline reservations.
  Essential: The executives *planning to attend the conference* must register in advance.

- *Prepositional*

  Nonessential: Ring number 555, *in the back of the case*, is available in yellow gold.
  Essential: The ring *in the back of the case* is available in yellow gold.

Note: The stock number identifies the ring adequately; the prepositional phrase *in the back of the case* is nonessential in the sentence containing the stock number. Commas are necessary. In the second sentence, however, the same prepositional phrase (*in the back of the case*) is *essential* to proper identification of the ring. Commas are *not* necessary.

- Phrases introduced by *in addition to, as well as, accompanied by*, etc., are nonessential; they are set off by commas.

   The teachers, as well as those students who were present, were introduced.

Contrasting expressions. *Contrasting expressions*, frequently introduced by *not* or *but*, are nonessential; they are set off by commas—unless they do not interrupt the flow of the sentences.

- **Interrupting the flow:**

   Cheese, not catsup, is the proper condiment for spaghetti.

- **Not interrupting the flow:**

   The player was tall but agile.
   The odor was pronounced but not overwhelming.

Appositives. An *appositive* is a noun (or group of words used as a noun) that follows and renames another noun in the sentence. Appositives are subject to the general rules for interrupting elements: set off *nonessential* appositives with commas; do not set off *essential* appositives with commas.

- **Nonessential:** Ms. Conhagen, *our teacher*, is the lecturer.

- **Essential:** John Wayne *the actor* starred in many pictures; John Wayne *the physician* is my neighbor.

   Note: In the first example, the name identifies the person adequately. The appositive *our teacher* is helpful, but nonessential. Commas are required. In the second example, there are two John Waynes. The appositives *the actor* and *the physician* are essential. Commas are not required.

Clarifiers. Other *clarifiers* are set off with commas if they interrupt the flow of the sentence.

- **Geographic:** The Colonel, a Californian, addressed the group.
   The defendant, residing at 1403 Central Avenue, denied guilt.

- **Association:** The speaker, chief accountant for the Bayview Corporation, talked briefly.
   The operator, a member of the safety club, drove very carefully.

- **Dates:** The third change dated 1875 was the most important.

The fact that commas are not used indicates that *dated 1875* is *essential* to identifying the most important change.

| 1874 Change | 1875 Change 1 | 1875 Change 2 | 1875 Change 3 | ←—Most Important |

The third change, dated 1875, was most important.

The commas indicate that *dated 1875* is *nonessential*. Since there is only one Change 3, that label is sufficient identification.

| 1873 Change 1 | 1874 Change 2 | 1875 Change 3 | ←——Most Important |

Note: The day of the *week* (as well as the day of the *month*) should be followed by a comma when both appear as part of the same date.

> It happened on Monday, May 6, 1776.

321   Separating Main Clauses

A comma may be used to separate main clauses joined by *coordinating conjunctions* (*and, but, for, nor, or, so,* and *yet*).

• *Compound sentence* (two main clauses).

> The typewriter is a valuable instrument of communication, but the telephone is faster.

Note: The comma may be omitted when both clauses are short and the omission does not decrease clarity.

> One held the lantern and the other chopped the wood.

• A *compound-complex sentence* is created by adding one or more dependent clauses to a compound sentence.

> The typewriter, *which is considered a relatively recent invention*, is a valuable instrument of communication, but the telephone is faster.

First, use a comma *to separate the two main clauses* before the coordinating conjunction (*but,* in this case). Second, use the commas necessary *to punctuate each of the main clauses.*

Note: A semicolon may be used between the main clauses of a compound or compound-complex sentence. See ¶ 365.

322   Separating Words, Phrases, and Clauses in Series

A comma is placed after each item (except the last) in a series of three or more items.

> The artist sketched trees, a cow, and a barn.

A comma is used after *etc., and so on, and so forth*, or a similar phrase at the end of a series—unless the sentence ends at that point.

> The artist sketched cows, chickens, pigs, etc., and then began to paint.
> The artist sketched cows, chickens, pigs, etc.

If there are only two items in the series—or if each item is preceded by *and, or,* or *nor*—a comma is *not* used to separate the items.

> The artist sketched cows and pigs.
> The artist sketched cows and pigs and horses.

The items in series may be phrases or clauses.

> A red barn, two tall trees, and four ducks were in the picture.
> Complete the set-up, run the test, and record the results.

Coordinate adjectives in a series. Commas are used to separate *coordinate adjectives* in a series.

- Adjectives in a series are coordinate if they each modify the noun independently.

  > There stands a happy, outgoing, vivacious person!

- Adjectives in a series are *not* coordinate if each modifies the total concept that follows.

  > They planned a surprise happy birthday party.

Business names. Some business firms prefer to omit some or all of the commas that would normally appear in their firm names. In addressing or referring to them, one should observe their preferences.

> Merrill Lynch, Pierce, Fenner & Smith Incorporated

If the firm's preference is unknown, employ the comma conventionally.

> Marrero, Young, Weiler, and Company

Repeated verbs. Use a comma to separate repeated verbs—those that are identical and are placed next to each other.

> When you work, work hard; when you play, play hard.

323   Other Uses of the Comma

Afterthoughts. An *afterthought*—an element added loosely or informally at the end of a sentence—is set off by a comma.

The star performer is third from the end, I think.

Omitted words. An omitted word or omitted words may be replaced by a comma.

The good fruit is on the top; the bad, on the bottom. (The second comma replaces the words *fruit is* .)

Personal names. In earlier times, it was considered *necessary* to use commas in personal or business names followed by abbreviations or numerals. The newer style is to omit many such commas but to respect the preferences of organizations and individuals by addressing them as *they* write their own personal and organizational names.

	Old Style	*New Style*
Jr.:	Laffan Wolfe, Jr.	Laffan Wolfe Jr.
Sr.:	Raphael Balise, Sr.	Raphael Balise Sr.
Roman Numerals:	Morato Crowley, III	Morato Crowley III
Arabic Numerals:	McErlean Elgin, 2d	McErlean Elgin 2d
Academic Degrees:	Susan Friede, B.A.	Susan Friede B.A.
Honorary Titles:	Austin Poag, Esq.	Austin Poag Esq.
Religious Orders:	Andre Tumpson, S.J.	Andre Tumpson S.J.
Incorporated:	Paprocki, Inc.	Paprocki Inc.
Limited:	Kiser, Ltd.	Kiser Ltd.

The comma in numbers.

One, two, or three digits:	1 21	131
Four digits:	9555	or 9,555
Four digits, appearing with larger numbers:	9,555	and 42,397
Five or more digits:	132,567	2,839,429

(For other conventions used in expressing numbers, see Unit 7.)

324   Typewriter Spacing with the Comma

	Before	*After*
• In normal use within the sentence.	0	1
• Followed by a closing quotation mark.	0	0
• In a number.	0	0

325   The Comma with Other Punctuation

- Dash, ¶ 328.
- Parentheses, ¶ 342.
- Quotation marks, ¶¶ 353, 354, 364.

DASH

326 **Break in thought.** Use a dash—or two—to indicate an abrupt break in thought.

> The small club—four feet long—was ready for use.
> The kicker eyed the ball warily—but with confidence.

Interrupted sentence. A dash may be used to indicate that a sentence has been broken off or interrupted.

> I think the real reason is— But one can never be sure in a case like this.

Note: If the interrupted sentence is a statement, the dash is followed by two spaces. No other punctuation is necessary. If the interrupted sentence is a question or exclamation, use the appropriate punctuation mark (? or !) followed by two spaces.

> Did you know that the real reason is—? But one can never be sure in a case like this.
> If you had only known that the real reason is—! But one can never be sure in a case like this.

Replacing commas. To *emphasize* a nonessential element, set it off with dashes instead of commas—or with a single dash if the nonessential element is at the end of the sentence.

> The emerald—a sparkling deep green mass—is the largest in the world.
> The last contestant won the grand prize—a new convertible!

Replacing a colon. When a strong but informal break is desired, use a dash instead of a colon to introduce introductory or explanatory elements.

> Some commodities are almost as liquid as gold—platinum, for instance.

Replacing a semicolon. When a strong but informal break is desired, use a dash instead of a semicolon between independent clauses.

> That is the way things used to be—they are better now.

Replacing parentheses. When strong emphasis is desired, use dashes instead of parentheses to set off a nonessential element.

> Giant redwoods—the largest trees in the world—grace California's northern slopes.

Emphasizing a single word.

> Fame—that is what they seek!
> They seek one thing—fame—above all else!
> There is only one thing they seek—fame!

Restatement.

> It was a rare steak—as rare a steak as I have ever seen.
> The mountain—that incredibly high mountain—won again.

Hesitation.

> We will be finished—well, nearly finished—by then.
> There are good reasons—several of them, I think—for that course of action.

With a summary or appositive. Use a dash before a summary or appositive when additional emphasis is required.

- Summary:

> Rubber bands, stationery, paper clips, envelopes—all are usually found in the desk.

> **But:** Rubber bands, stationery, paper clips, and envelopes are usually found in the desk. (Do not use a dash if the summarizing word [all] is not the subject.)

- Appositive:

> Mr. Lincoln—the president—returned the stare.
> The stare was returned by Mr. Lincoln—the president.

With quotations. Use a dash before the source of a quotation.

> Remember that time is money.
> —Benjamin Franklin

327   Typewriter Spacing with the Dash

	Before	*After*
• In normal use.	0	0
• Following a broken-off statement.	0	2
• Following the question mark at the end of a broken-off question.	0	2
• Following the exclamation mark at the end of a broken-off exclamation.	0	2

328   The Dash with Other Punctuation

Before an opening dash, use no punctuation except a period following an abbreviation.

Not: They came as quickly as could be expected,—and quietly.

But: They came as quickly as could be expected—and quietly.

And: She prefers not to use the title *Mrs.*—unless absolutely necessary.

When a question or exclamation within a sentence is set off by dashes, use a question mark or exclamation mark before the closing dash.

> The new show—is it tonight?—opens in the old theater.
> You'll have to wait here—stop that truck!—until the other truck is unloaded.

Note: A *declarative sentence*—statement or command—set off by dashes is not followed by a *period*.

Not: The house we will visit—it is the large frame house at the end of the street.—has 22 exterior doors.

But: The house we will visit—it is the large frame house at the end of the street—has 22 exterior doors.

When a closing dash falls at the end of a sentence, it is *replaced* by the end-of-sentence punctuation—period, question mark, or exclamation mark.

> Put the pieces in the box—quickly, if you please.
> I believe we leave at ten o'clock—or is it eleven?
> The players were there—all six of them!

When a closing dash conflicts with a comma, retain the dash—eliminating the comma.

> You may think your answer is acceptable—even correct—but it is neither.

Not: You may think your answer is acceptable—even correct—, but it is neither.

Not: You may think your answer is acceptable—even correct,—but it is neither.

When a closing dash conflicts with a colon, semicolon, or closing parenthesis, eliminate the closing dash and use the required punctuation—colon, semicolon, or closing parenthesis.

- **Colon replaces closing dash:**

> This is our most successful model—based on current sales figures: the 2K14 engine on the SXL42 frame.

- **Semicolon replaces closing dash:**

  Add the stripe—the wide one between the wheel housings; it will give the side view the appearance of motion.

- **Closing parenthesis replaces closing dash:**

  Use the darker color (green would be my first choice—it blends well with the top color) on the bottom.

DIAGONAL (SLANT, SLASH, VIRGULE)

329   **Indicating choice.** The diagonal may indicate a choice:

> Eggs and/or bacon will be served.
>   Meaning that the choices are:
>   Eggs and bacon
>   Eggs
>   Bacon
>
> Bird and/or Tex will go.
>   Meaning that Bird and Tex will go
>   or
>   Bird will go
>   or
>   Tex will go.

Note: Many writers believe that this form should be confined to tables, technical data, etc., where abbreviations are appropriate—not used generally. Acceptable substitutes are:

> Eggs or bacon (or both) will be served.
> Bird or Tex, or both of them, will go.

In business letters. The diagonal is sometimes used between the initials of the originator and those of the typist in the reference sections of business letters.

> LIF/crh   lif/crh   LIF/CRH

With poetry. Lines of poetry quoted within a sentence or paragraph may be separated from one another by diagonals. Space before and after the diagonal. If more than two lines of poetry are quoted, space the lines as they are in the original poem—or single-space and start all lines of the poem five spaces right of the left margin.

> The reference was: "An arrow, flaming from the eastern sky / to blaze in radiant arch, and die. . . ."

In fractions. The diagonal is used to type fractions not on the type-writer keyboard.

5/8　　　3/4　　　15/38　　　19/64　　　327/519

Note: Do not mix *made* fractions (1/2, 1/4, 3/16, etc.) and *keyboard* fractions (½, ¼, etc.) in the same sentence.

In technical material. In tables, bills, technical work, etc., the diagonal may be used to abbreviate the words *with* and *without*.

with trim	without wheels	coffee with cream
w/trim	w/o wheels	coffee w/cream

330　　**Typewriter Spacing with the Diagonal**

	Before	After
• Separating two lines (no more) of poetry quoted within a paragraph or sentence.	1	1
• All other uses.	0	0

ELLIPSIS

331　　See ¶¶ 360, 361.

EXCLAMATION MARK

332　　Use the exclamation mark after an appropriate element of a sentence—or at the end of a sentence—to indicate

- **Irony:**　　　Another "accident!" What a coincidence!
- **Dissent:**　　They call it a free(!) society.

Note: If the exclamation mark falls at a point at which there is not a

natural break in the sentence, enclose the exclamation mark in
parentheses. This format applies to *all* uses of the exclamation
mark within the sentence—not just to its use to indicate dissent.

- **Amusement:**   Well, easy come, easy go!

- **Urgency:**   Hurry! We'll be late.

- **Surprise:**   Oh! You startled me.

- **Disbelief:**   Worry! You call that a worry?

- **Enthusiasm:**   Wonderful! Wonderful performance!

- **Other Strong
  Feeling:**   Stop that!

Elliptical expressions. Exclamation marks are frequently used at
the ends of *elliptical expressions*—short expressions that are
used as sentences.

Full Sentence: That is fantastic! What a show it was!
Elliptical: Fantastic! What a show!

Full Sentence: You hurry! You hurry! You hurry! The show is
                            about to begin.
Elliptical: Hurry! Hurry! Hurry! The show is about to begin.

333   Typewriter Spacing with the Exclamation Mark

	Before	*After*
• Ending a sentence.	0	2
• Enclosed in parentheses.	0	0
Opening parenthesis before an exclamation mark.	0	0
Closing parenthesis after an exclamation mark.	0	1
• Within a sentence, followed directly by another punctuation mark.	0	0
• Within a sentence, not followed directly by another punctuation mark.	0	0

334   The Exclamation Mark with Other Punctuation

- Dash, ¶ 328.

- Parentheses, ¶ 342.

- Quotation marks, ¶¶ 352, 364.

HYPHEN

335   Compound Words

Compound nouns. Compound nouns follow no regular patterns. Some are written solid, some are spaced, and some are hyphenated. Consult a dictionary.

- **Solid:**   The *timetable* is explicit.   The *dropout* looked for work.

- **Spaced:**   Finish the *time study*.   Check the *sales slip*.

- **Hyphenated:** Take a *time-out* early.   Some *know-how* is needed.

Verb phrases. *Verb phrases* may resemble compound nouns. Verb phrases, however, are treated as separate words.

Some students will *drop out.*
We will lose money if *sales slip.*
They do not *know how.*

Compound verbs. *Compound verbs* are usually hyphenated or written solid.

Double-space the manuscript.
Proofread the first chapter.

Gerunds. A *gerund* (the *ing* form of a verb that functions as a noun—*running, talking,* etc.) that is compound requires a hyphen only if that gerund is followed by an object.

a free-running *gear*
a gear that is free running

a thirst-quenching *drink*
a drink that is thirst quenching

Compound adjectives. A *compound adjective* shown in the dictionary as hyphenated is always hyphenated when used immediately before a noun, unless it is a comparative or superlative form.

a *high-level* meeting   some *worn-out* machinery
some *high-priced* goods   the *tax-exempt* bonds

But: a *higher level* meeting
a *highest level* meeting

Note: When the same form is used elsewhere in a sentence, *do not* use a hyphen.

- **Hyphen not needed:**   a meeting at a high level
                             the machinery is worn out

Compound words with a common base. If two or more related compound words have a common base, use *suspending hyphens* rather than repeat the base word.

Not: 1-jewel, 12-jewel, and 17-jewel watches

But: 1-, 12-, and 17-jewel watches

Note: If a suspended hyphen is not followed by another punctuation mark, one space must be left after the hyphen.

    1- and 2-jewel watches

Improvised words. *Improvised words* may be formed using the hyphen.

The *Y-shaped* intersection needs a traffic signal.
They carved a *jack-o-lantern.*

336   Prefixes and Suffixes

Generally, a hyphen is *not* used to separate a prefix or suffix from the base word.

Prefix or Suffix Shown in Caps	Word is Written Like This	Not Like This
DEcentralize	decentralize	de-centralize
ILlegal	illegal	il-legal
INdirect	indirect	in-direct
publishING	publishing	publish-ing
waterPROOF	waterproof	water-proof
initiaTION	initiation	initia-tion

Double vowels; triple consonants. A hyphen is sometimes used to avoid double vowels or triple consonants.

This	Not This
anti-intellectual	antiintellectual
semi-independent	semiindependent
re-echo	reecho
thrill-less	thrillless
shell-like	shelllike

But: coordinate   reelect   preempt

After "re." Use a hyphen after the prefix *re* (meaning *again*) when necessary to avoid confusion with other words spelled the same way.

recover a loss	re-cover a cushion
reform and perfect	re-form into a group
recollect an incident	re-collect a returned collection

After "self." Use a hyphen after *self* when employing it as a prefix.

self-educated   self-imposed   self-denial

But: Omit the hyphen when employing *self* as a base word to which a suffix is attached.

selfhood   selfsame   selfish

Root words beginning with a capital letter. When a root word begins with a capital letter, a hyphen usually follows the prefix.

re-Americanize   trans-Canadian   pre-World War II

But: transatlantic   transalpine   transpacific

Family relationship words. In words describing family relationships, follow these patterns:

- great (hyphen)   great-grandmother   great-aunt
- grand (solid)   grandmother   grandchild
- step (solid)   stepfather   stepchild
- in-law (hyphen)   father-in-law   sister-in-law

337   Other Uses of the Hyphen

Company names. In company names, use hyphens exactly as the firm does on its letterhead and in its literature.

Elgin-Webb, Slick and Company   McFarlane-Norato

Numeric and alphabetic ranges. Use the hyphen to identify numeric and alphabetic ranges.

1-20	(1 through 20)
21-99	(21 through 99)
A-E	(A through E)
in-inventory	(*in* through *inventory* alphabetically)

Note: The hyphen is usually typed solid when used to express numeric ranges. It is sometimes set off with spaces when used to express alphabetic ranges.

1-9   22-256   Ar - Bl   A - M

338   Typewriter Spacing with the Hyphen

	Before	*After*
• In normal use (compound words, etc.).	0	0
• Suspended (¶ 335).	0	0 or 1
• Numeric ranges (¶ 337).	0	0
• Alphabetic ranges (¶ 337).	0	0
• Alphabetic ranges, alternate method.	1	1

PARENTHESES

339   Parentheses Setting Off Nonessential Elements

Parentheses are used to set off nonessential elements. While commas or dashes can serve the same general purpose, parentheses are appropriate for the *least* essential explanations, qualifications, or digressions.

The chairs (about five of them, I think) were in a circle.

Dashes raise the reading voice to a shout, emphasizing the element they set off. Dashes may set off essential or nonessential elements—but they always *emphasize.*

Nonessential: The chairs—five of them—were arranged in a circle.
Essential: One principle—the golden rule—guided their decisions.

Commas lower the reading voice, indicating that the enclosed element is nonessential.

The golden rule, an important principle, guides them.

Parentheses lower the reading voice to a whisper, seeming to apologize for intruding with information so nonessential.

The golden rule (Matthew 7:12) guides their decisions.

Parenthetical elements are nonessential elements enclosed in parentheses. A parenthetical element may be a word (number, figure, symbol, etc.), a phrase, a clause, or a sentence.

Their flight (923) is departing.
This typewriter has large (pica) type.
The smaller type (12 characters to the inch) is elite.
The larger type (it is called "pica") is easy to read.

The larger type is easier to read. (It is called "pica" type.)

340   Parentheses Replacing Commas and Dashes

Commas. Parentheses may replace commas when parentheses add clarity.

Not: The weather, rain, sleet, and hail, caused the delay.
But: The weather (rain, sleet, and hail) caused the delay.
 Or: The weather: rain, sleet, and hail, caused the delay.

Not: The address, 555 Park Shore Drive, Columbus, Ohio, is correct.
But: The address (555 Park Shore Drive, Columbus, Ohio) is correct.

Dashes. Parentheses may replace dashes in setting off *nonessential* elements.

The larger locomotive—a steam engine—could pull the load.
(*A steam engine* is a nonessential element; the dashes emphasize it.)

The larger locomotive (a steam engine) could pull the load.
(The parentheses de-emphasize the nonessential element.)

The locomotive—with a diesel engine—could pull the load.
(*With a diesel engine* is an essential element—parentheses should not replace the dashes.)

341   Parentheses Organizing Data

Outlines. Parentheses may be used to enclose numbers or letters identifying certain sections of an outline.

```
I. _____
   A. _____
      1. _____
         a. _____
            (1) _____
               (a) _____
                  1) _____
                     a) _____
```

Enumerations. Numbers or letters organizing an enumeration may be enclosed in parentheses.

Try this procedure: (1) Lie flat on your back. (2) Breathe deeply. (3) Raise your feet slowly.
Pick up these materials: (a) three ballpoint pens, (b) one typewriter ribbon, (c) a ream of carbon paper.

Numeric information. Detailed nonessential numeric information is frequently enclosed in parentheses—particularly confirming (restated) data in law documents.

- **Dates:**   The new charter was issued at the time of the reorganiza-
              tion (1902).

- **Time:**   That is four (4) months after the first payment.

- **Amount:**   You now owe One Thousand Two Hundred and Fifteen
              Dollars ($1,215).

- **References:**   These items are also held in trust (see Clause 27, page 12
              of the supplement).

342   Parentheses with Other Punctuation

Punctuation before an opening parenthesis. Before an opening
parenthesis, never use a comma, semicolon, colon, or dash. If an
entire sentence is parenthetical, the previous sentence is
punctuated normally: there may be a period, question mark, or
exclamation mark (followed by two spaces) before the opening
parenthesis.

> There may be a typist available today. (If so, the project can proceed
> on schedule.)

Punctuation after an opening parenthesis. After an opening parenthesis, use no punctuation.

Note: Do not capitalize the first letter after an opening parenthesis unless
it begins a complete parenthetical sentence standing alone—not a
parenthetical sentence within a sentence.

> The tree (it is an elm) may survive.
> The tree may survive. (It is an elm.)

Unless: The first letter following the opening parenthesis would be
capitalized *anywhere* in the sentence (proper noun,
proper adjective, the pronoun *I*).

> The tree (I believe it is an elm) may survive.

Punctuation before a closing parenthesis. Before a closing parenthesis, do not use a period unless:

- The parenthetical expression ends with an abbreviation.

> The Orr family (of Fifth Ave.) will move tomorrow.

- The entire sentence is parenthetical.

> The Orr family will move tomorrow. (They live on Fifth Avenue.)

Do not use a question mark or quotation mark before a closing
parenthesis unless the mark:

- applies only to a parenthetical element that is part of a longer sentence, and

- is different from the punctuation mark used at the end of the sentence

Not: Does the new jacket (is it a red one?) fit properly?
But: Does the new jacket (is it a red one) fit properly?
And: Does the new jacket (it is a red one!) fit properly?

Not: Now that's a jacket (it's a red one!) that fits!
But: Now that's a jacket (it's a red one) that fits!

Do not use a comma, semicolon, colon, or dash before a closing parenthesis.

> The book (the yellow one with the soft cover), as thick as it is, is incomplete.

> Type page 1 again (not the title page); it must be perfect.

> Three sizes will fit (not four): 8, 10, and 12.

> The leaves will fall—in the autumn (or fall, if you prefer)—as they always have.

Punctuation after a closing parenthesis.

- If a parenthetical element ends the sentence, place the end-of-sentence punctuation *outside* the closing parenthesis.

> We will leave Sunday (tomorrow).
> Will you be with us Sunday (tomorrow)?
> We cannot leave until Sunday (tomorrow)!

- If the parenthetical element does *not* end the sentence, punctuate normally after the closing parenthesis.

- If the entire sentence is parenthetical, use *no* punctuation after the closing parenthesis; place the end-of-sentence punctuation before the closing parenthesis.

> (They live on Fifth Avenue.)

Punctuation enclosed by parentheses. Parentheses may be used to enclose:

- A question mark to express doubt.

> They were offered a perfect(?) diamond for $500.

- An exclamation mark to emphasize a word or other element.

> They were offered a perfect(!) diamond for $500.

Use brackets to enclose a parenthetical expression within a parenthetical expression. See ¶ 312.

We know that the incident actually occurred (the date [1812] is more difficult to establish).

343   Typewriter Spacing with Parentheses

Opening Parenthesis:	*Before*	*After*
• Parenthetical matter is *not* a free-standing sentence.	1	0
• Parenthetical matter *is* a free-standing sentence.	2	0
• Parenthetical matter immediately precedes a question mark or exclamation mark.	0	0
Closing Parenthesis:		
• Following parenthetical matter within a sentence.	0	1
• Following normal end-of-sentence punctuation.	0	2
• Followed by another punctuation mark.	0	0

PERIOD

344   Period Following a Sentence

Use a period at the end of a sentence that

- **States:**   The time is 0830.
- **Asserts:**   I believe that solution is best.
- **Requests:**   Please provide your name and address.
- **Commands:**   Close the door at once.

An *elliptical sentence* is a sentence shortened by omitting words that are *understood*. Use the same sentence-end punctuation for elliptical sentences as you would if the sentences were complete.

- **Question:**   Do you like ice cream?
- **Answer Using Complete Sentences:** Do I like ice cream? Yes, I do! I particularly like coconut ice cream in a sugar cone.

- **Answer Using Elliptical Sentences:**   Do I? Yes! Particularly coconut in a sugar cone.

Indirect questions. A period is used to mark the end of an indirect question.

> They asked if the weather will change tomorrow.
> I question whether the presumption is valid.

Requests, instructions, and commands. Use a period after requests, instructions, orders, and commands that are

- Not expected to raise questions.

- Written with the expectation of compliance.

- Written as requests only to soften the communication.

> Will you please submit the report in the usual manner.

Note: If it is desirable to soften the message further, it may be worded as a question *and* followed by a question mark.

> Will you please submit the report in the usual manner?

Run-in headings. A period or other appropriate end-of-sentence punctuation is used after a run-in heading. A *run-in heading*

- Starts at the left margin or is indented; it is the left-most item on the line.

- Is followed by text material or a free-standing heading.

> **Courtesy.** Another positive quality that an office worker should cultivate is courtesy.

Listed items. Listed items may be identified by letters or numbers followed by periods. Single or double parentheses *may* enclose or follow identifying letters or numbers on lists—and *should* be used in certain sections of outlines. See ¶ 341.

1.	Manuscript paper	A.	Manuscript paper
2.	Typewriter ribbons	B.	Typewriter ribbons
3.	Correction fluid	C.	Correction fluid

Enumerations should be typed in the following manner:

1. Single-space within each item.

2. Double-space between items.

3. Leave two spaces after the period following the identifying letter or number before each item.

The use of periods at the ends of lines should be consistent. When a lead element is followed by an enumeration, periods may be

1. Used at the end of each item.

2. Used at the ends of all lines that constitute sentences or elliptical sentences, treating the lead element as an understood part of each sentence or elliptical sentence.

3. Used at the end of the last line, treating the entire enumeration as a sentence.

345   Periods Following Abbreviations

Many abbreviations are written with periods following each letter or word. Do not space after periods within an abbreviation; space after the final period, as though the abbreviation were a word and the period were the final letter in that word.

Mrs.	c.o.d.	Lt.	B.S.
Dr.	Ph.D.	U.S.A.	M.A.
f.o.b.	W.Va.	Col.	A.S.

Many other abbreviations are written without periods; some, like USA, are written *with* or *without* periods. A dictionary is the best source for checking a specific abbreviation.

sq in   COD   rpm   mph

Note: If an abbreviation followed by a period ends a sentence, do not add another period to mark the end of the sentence—the period at the end of the abbreviation serves both purposes.

Not: It is part of the U.S.A.. If the territory . . .

But: It is part of the U.S.A. If the territory . . .

And: . . . marks the territory (it is part of the U.S.A.). If the territory . . .

If an abbreviation followed by a period ends a question or exclamation, use a question mark or exclamation mark *in addition to* the period following the abbreviation.

Was the meeting scheduled for 7:30 p.m.?
The items were definitely to be sent c.o.d.!

Acronyms. Most *acronyms* (words made of the initials of other words) are written in capital letters without periods.

Volunteers in Service to America (VISTA)
National Organization of Women (NOW)
World Health Organization (WHO)

Note: When an acronym utilizes more than the initial letter of any word, it is usually written in lowercase letters—the first letter only being capitalized.

Hamilton County Agencies, Inc. (Hamco, Inc.)

Contractions. Contractions are not followed by periods (unless they are at the ends of sentences).

I'm sure you can.   We'll try again.   They can't.

346   Periods as Decimal Points

Use the period as a decimal point.

$5.55   .33   1.5 sq in $100.00

347   Typewriter Spacing with the Period

	Before	*After*
• Ending a sentence.	0	2
• After an abbreviation within a sentence.	0	1
• After a number or letter indicating enumeration.	0	2
• When followed by another punctuation mark (comma, closing parenthesis, closing quotation mark).	0	0
• As a decimal.	0	0

348   The Period with Other Punctuation

- Dash, ¶ 328.
- Parentheses, ¶ 342.
- Quotation mark, ¶¶ 352, 353, 364.

QUESTION MARK

349   Use a question mark to indicate a direct question.

Will you be there?

Use a question mark to indicate an *elliptical* (shortened) question.

> You? (In the context of a conversation or with explanatory gestures
>   meaning: Will you be there?)
> Enough? (Is that enough?)

The voice may rise to indicate that what is worded as a statement is really a question. The question mark identifies the "statement" as a question.

> *That's* the winning entry?
> You *called*?

A question at the beginning of a longer sentence may be

- Followed by a question mark.

> How can the problem be solved? is the question.

- Followed by a comma.

> How can the problem be solved, is the question.

- Converted to an indirect question.

> The question is how the problem can be solved.

Questions within a sentence. A short question within a longer sentence may be set off with commas if it converts the longer sentence into a question. The longer sentence, having become a question, is followed by a question mark.

> It is true, is it not, that the show was a success?

But: If the short question falls at the end of the longer sentence:

> It is true that the show was a success, is it not?

A question at the end of a longer question may be introduced using a

- **Comma:**   The question is, Was the show a success?
- **Colon:**   The question is: Was the show a success?

Note: A colon is preferable if the introductory element is an independent clause.

> The question was finally asked: Is the show a success?

Series of questions. A series of brief questions having the same subject and verb may be:

- Treated as a single sentence, using question marks.

> Would you like cake? pie? ice cream?

- Treated as a single sentence, using commas.

  Would you like cake, pie, ice cream?

- Treated as a series of separate, sometimes elliptical (shortened) questions.

  Would you like cake? Pie? Ice cream?

Note: If the questions do not share the same subject and verb, they must be treated as a series of independent questions.

  Is the game over? Did we win? Was it close?

Question marks within parentheses. A question mark enclosed in parentheses may be inserted at any appropriate point within a sentence to express uncertainty or doubt.

  It began in the winter(?) of 1774.
  The negative(?) wire should be grounded.

No question mark. Do not use a question mark:

- After an indirect question.

  They asked if you know the answer.

- After a request or command unless you intend to imply the option of refusal.

  Option to refuse: Will you please close the door?
  No **option to refuse:**   Will you please close the door.

350   **Typewriter Spacing with the Question Mark**

	Before	*After*
• Ending a sentence.	0	2
• Enclosed in parentheses.	0	0
• Within a sentence; not followed directly by another punctuation mark.	0	1
• Within a sentence; followed directly by another punctuation mark.	0	0

351   **The Question Mark with Other Punctuation**

- Dash, ¶ 328.

- Parentheses, ¶ 342.

- Quotation marks, ¶¶ 352, 355, 364.

QUOTATION MARKS

352   Enclosing Direct Quotations

Quotation marks are used to enclose the *exact* words of a direct quotation.

- **Direct quotation**
  Use quotation marks: "Block that kick," they shouted.

- **Indirect quotation**   They shouted for the team to block that
  Do not use quotation marks: kick.

- **Selective direct quotation**   The coach said that the team should
  Use quotation marks: "block that kick."

                                    (The coach *actually* said "You must re-
                                    member to block that kick.")

                          Not: The coach said *"that the team should*
                                    block that kick." (The coach did not
                                    say the italicized words.)

A quotation may consist of a

- **Statement:**   "The water is warm."

- **Exclamation:**   "Fly the flag!"

- **Question:**   "What is the time?"

When a direct quotation stands alone (as do the examples above), the end-of-sentence punctuation is placed *inside* the closing quotation mark.

Around the words *yes* and *no*. Do not use quotation marks around the words *yes* and *no* unless there is a need to emphasize the fact that they are the exact words of the speaker or writer.

        If the boss says yes, let's leave at once.
But: It is obvious that the producer enjoys saying "no."

Around well-known sayings. Do not use quotation marks around well-known phrases, mottos, proverbs, sayings, etc.

        That proves that a stitch in time saves nine.

353   Beginning a Sentence

When a quotation begins a sentence, it may:

- Require a comma—or the retention of a question mark or exclamation mark.

  "The water is warm," the lifeguard said.
  "Fly the flag!" said the drum major.
  "What is the time?" asked the announcer.

- Be woven into the sentence and therefore not require following punctuation.

  "The water is warm" came as welcome news.

In either case, the period at the end of the quoted sentence is eliminated; a question mark or exclamation mark is not.

354 Within a Sentence

A quotation may be woven into a sentence so that no hesitation—and therefore no comma—is required.

Saying "Please" will not hurt you.

Essential elements. A quotation that is an essential element is *not* set off with commas.

The song that begins "Oh beautiful, for spacious skies" is not the national anthem.

Note: The voice *rises* on an *essential* element, *falls* on a *nonessential* element.

Nonessential elements. A quotation that is a nonessential element is set off with commas.

The first four words of the national anthem, "Oh, say can you see," are familiar to most Americans.

See note above on essential and nonessential elements.
Words like *he said, she said*, etc., are treated as nonessential elements; they *are* set off by commas.

The deliverer said, "That dog has a long tail and bites hard."
"That dog has a long tail," the deliverer said, "and bites hard."
"That dog has a long tail and bites hard," the deliverer said.

355 Ending a Sentence

When a quotation ends a sentence and is introduced by an expression such as *he said* or *she said*, that expression is usually followed by a comma.

The lifeguard said, "The water is warm."
The drum major said, "Fly the flag!"
The announcer asked, "What is the time?"

Note: The introductory comma may be omitted if the quotation is short and blends smoothly into the sentence.

> The seller finally said "Please."

If the intent is to emphasize the quotation, the comma may remain—or a dash may be used.

> The seller finally said, "Please."
> The seller finally said—"Please."

If the introductory expression is an independent clause, a colon should be used instead of the introductory comma.

> The seller finally said the magic word: "Please."

356 Long Quotations

A quotation of four or more typed lines should be indented five spaces from *both* margins and single-spaced. When a quotation consists of more than one sentence *or* is single-spaced and indented from both margins as an extract, the introductory expression is followed by a colon.

- **Two Sentences:**   They shouted again and again: "We want the coach! We want the coach!"

- **Extract:**   Franklin's recommendation was:
      As to their studies, it would be well if they could be taught everything that is useful and everything that is ornamental. But art is long and their time is short. It is therefore proposed that they learn those things most useful and most ornamental, regard being had to the several professions for which they are intended.

Note: Quotation marks are not used when the quotation is indented from both margins.

Dialogue. In dialogue and conversation, a new paragraph should begin each time a new speaker speaks.

> "That is the best tire we have," the tire seller said.
> "But is it sturdy?" the customer asked.
> "This tire," responded the tire seller, "is as sturdy as they come."

357 Quoting (Reproducing) Without Using Quotation Marks

Letters, reports, etc. Letters, reports, tables, etc., that are too lengthy to quote are frequently photocopied and attached to or distributed with more comprehensive letters, reports, etc. When this procedure is followed, they should be clearly identified as *copies* of the original, and the 1978 Copyright Law should be reviewed to make certain that the copying is not in violation.

Poetry. Poetry may be quoted by

- Reproducing the entire poem or part of the poem.
- Typing the poem as an extract. See ¶ 356.
- Typing each stanza as a paragraph.

Plays, scripts, and court testimony. In plays, scripts, and court testimony, each speaker is identified. This makes the use of quotation marks unnecessary.

> Detective: This is the murder weapon!
> Suspect: That puny little thing?
> Detective: Yes, it is more lethal than it looks.

358   **Quotation Marks for Special Emphasis**

Quotation marks may be used to indicate purposely ungrammatical or other unusual expressions that need special emphasis because they incorporate humor, irony, whimsy, slang, coined words, or purposely awkward or "incorrect" construction.

> The appearance of the job indicated that the mechanic had mastered the "takeaparts" and was still working on the "puttogethers."

Formal definitions. Formal definitions are sometimes enclosed in quotation marks; the word defined is then underscored or italicized.

> We shall use data to mean "organized information."

Foreign words. Foreign words are sometimes translated in the same manner as are formal definitions: the foreign word is underscored or italicized; the translation is enclosed in quotation marks.

> They live at 880 Rue de le Paix, "Street of the Peace."

Technical terms. The same form is used to introduce or define technical terms as for formal definitions—particularly in writing of a nontechnical nature.

> Every lever has a *fulcrum*, the "point of support on which the lever turns." The fulcrum of a seesaw is between the two riders: the point on which the seesaw board rests.

Note: After the term is introduced, it is used without special emphasis of any kind. It is *not* enclosed in quotation marks.

Words used as words. Words used *as words* rather than for their meanings may be enclosed in quotation marks. Underscoring or italicizing such words is a more frequently used convention, however. The same convention applies to letters, numbers, other characters, and groups of all of the above. See ¶ 368.

> Spell "correct" with a "c," not a "k."

Enclose words following the words *labeled, titled, marked, identified,* etc., in quotation marks when the exact message is quoted.

> The box was labeled "Fragile."
> The label identified the contents of the bottle as "Poison."

359   Using Brackets to Identify Insertions in Quoted Material

Note: See ¶¶ 312 and 313 for uses of brackets and hints on how to draw them.

360   Using Ellipses to Indicate Omissions in Quoted Material

Create the *ellipsis* by typing three periods with one space between each pair of periods: Period, Space, Period, Space, Period: . _ . _ .

Short omissions. Use the ellipsis to indicate short omissions in quoted material.

> "There is, I believe, an easier way."
> "There is _ . _ . _ . _ an easier way."

Note: Omit punctuation adjacent to the ellipsis *unless* such punctuation is necessary to the meaning or structure of the sentence. Commas are *not* needed in the example above; the semicolon *is* needed in the example below.

> "There is an easier way; . . . we may never find it."

Fragmentary quotation. The ellipsis may be used to indicate a fragmentary quotation.

> The coach said that the team should ". . . block that kick."

Omission at end of sentence. When an omission occurs at the end of a sentence, the ellipsis is followed by the normal end-of-sentence punctuation.

- **Period:**   "That is the question, printed precisely as stated."
                      "That is the question. . . ."

- **Exclamation**   "That is the question, printed precisely as stated!"
  Mark: "That is the question. . . !"

- **Question**   "Is that the exact question, precisely as stated?"
  Mark: "Is that the exact question . . . ?"

Omission of one or more sentences. If one or more sentences are omitted, use the ellipsis between quoted sentences at the point of omission.

- One or more sentences are omitted following this sentence! . . . The quotation is continued in this sentence.

- The sentence before the omission may end with a question mark. Is that so? . . . Yes, that is so.

- If the sentence before the omission ends with a period, type the ellipsis indicating that one or more sentences are omitted. . . . After the ellipsis, type the period, space twice, and continue typing.

Omission of one or more paragraphs. If one or more *paragraphs* are omitted, type an ellipsis at the point of omission as described above, and then continue the quotation like this:

This represents the last sentence in a quoted paragraph. . . .
    This represents the first sentence in the resumed quotation—also the beginning of a new paragraph. The ellipsis above indicates that something has been omitted—as little as a single sentence; as much as one or more paragraphs.

As an alternative, type three asterisks—centered on the page with one space between each pair of asterisks (type asterisk, space, asterisk, space, asterisk)—to indicate that one or more paragraphs are omitted.

This represents the last sentence in a quoted paragraph.

* * *

This represents the first sentence in the resumed quotation—also the beginning of a new paragraph. The three asterisks indicate the omission of one or more paragraphs. Leave a blank line above them and a blank line below them.

When ellipsis is unnecessary. If the quotation is short and blends into the sentence, an ellipsis is unnecessary.

If the engineer is correct, the unit will last "a year or more."

Displayed quotations. Normally, the ellipsis is not used to introduce a displayed quotation or extract.

The speaker said:

I am sure that this event marks a new beginning, undertaken on a day we shall remember, in a place we shall find impossible to forget.

If the displayed quotation begins *within* a quoted sentence, an ellipsis should be used.

> The speaker said:

> . . . this event marks a new beginning, undertaken on a day we shall remember, in a place we shall find impossible to forget.

Advertising material. Ellipses are sometimes used to connect loosely related words and phrases in advertising material.

> It takes two . . . two formulas . . . two ingredients . . . to get two great results!

361   Typewriter Spacing with the Ellipsis

	Before	After
• The ellipsis consists of three periods typed with one space between each pair of periods (. _ . _ .).		
• Within a sentence.	1	1
• Preceding a closing quotation mark.	1	0
• Preceding end-of-sentence punctuation.	1	1
• Following end-of-sentence punctuation.	1	2

362   Quotation Marks Identifying Literary and Artistic Works

Published works. Enclose the title of any *section* of a published work in quotation marks. The *published work* may be a book, play, symphony, etc.; the *section* may be a chapter, unit, lesson, etc. The *titles* of published works are usually *underscored* or *italicized.* See ¶ 368.

> The third unit in Reference Manual for Office Personnel is "Punctuation." (Unit in a published book.)

> The most popular column in *The Daily Bugle* is "Horse Sense." (Column in a newspaper.)

Unpublished works. Enclose the title of an unpublished work in quotation marks.

> My new book is called "What I Did on My Vacation Last Summer at Aunt Druscilla's Farm." (An unpublished book.)
> The latest report, "Cost of Data Acquisition," is revealing. (An unpublished report.)

Songs; radio and television shows. Enclose the title of a song, a radio or television *show*, a radio or television *series*, etc., in quotation marks.

> They sang "The Star Spangled Banner." (A song.)
> All the original "Perry Mason" shows were run at least three times. (A television series.)

363   Typewriter Spacing with Quotation Marks

Opening:	*Before*	*After*
• Beginning a sentence.	2	0
• Following a colon.	2	0
• Following a dash.	0	0
• Following an opening parenthesis.	0	0
• All other uses.	1	0
Closing:		
• Ending a sentence.	0	2
• Immediately preceding another punctuation mark.	0	0
• All other uses.	0	1

364   Quotation Marks with Other Punctuation

Use a single quotation mark (made with the apostrophe when typewriting) to identify a quotation within a quotation.

> The author said, "My new chapter is called 'Space.' "

Place a period or comma *inside* the closing quotation mark.

> The director said, "Run to the exit."
> "Run to the exit," said the director.

Place a colon or semicolon *outside* a closing quotation mark.

> The teacher said, "I shall repeat the instructions": but that was the last thing we heard.
> The duffer swung a golf "stick"; the golfer, a club.

When a quoted statement, question, or exclamation ends a sentence and is preceded by a statement, question, or exclamation, follow these patterns. Use an introductory comma if the quotation does not blend into the sentence.

> • Exclamation "Exclamation!" Do not shout "I will!"

- Exclamation "Question?"!   See "What Makes Sammy Run?"!

- Exclamation "Statement"!   You must see "As You Like It"!

- Question "Exclamation!"?   Did the driver shout "I will!"?

- Question "Question?"   Did you see "What Makes Sammy Run?"

- Question "Statement"?   Did you see "As You Like It"?

- Statement "Exclamation!"   The driver shouted "I will!"

- Statement "Question?"   We saw "What Makes Sammy Run?"

- Statement "Statement."   We saw "As You Like It."

SEMICOLON

365   A semicolon may be used to replace a coordinating conjunction between independent clauses. (*Coordinating conjunctions* are *and, but, for, or, nor,* and *so. Independent clauses* have a subject and verb and can stand alone as sentences.)

> The sun rises earlier and the days are warmer.
> The sun rises earlier; the days are warmer.

Note: Do not replace a coordinating conjunction with a comma.
Not: The sun rises earlier, the days are warmer.

Punctuation between independent clauses should be determined by the relationship between the clauses.

- **Closely Related:**

> The oil line broke, so the oil pressure dropped. (A strong break is not
>   required.)
> The oil line broke; the oil pressure dropped. (The coordinating conjunction is replaced by a semicolon.)

>   **Not:** The oil line broke, the oil pressure dropped. (Do not replace the
>   coordinating conjunction with a comma.)

- **Not Closely Related; Strongest Break Is Desirable:**

> They sat quietly thinking about the problem. Time passed slowly. (For
>   a stronger break in thought, punctuate the independent clauses as
>   separate sentences.)

- **Independent Clauses Containing Commas:**

> **Unclear:** I asked for lettuce, tomato, and mayonnaise, but I got

parsley, tartar sauce, and pickle. (The use of commas to separate items in a series *and* independent clauses in the same sentence is confusing.)

Better: I asked for lettuce, tomato, and mayonnaise; I got parsley, tartar sauce, and pickle. (Clearer, because the semicolon [between independent clauses] creates a stronger break than do the commas [between items in a series].)

- **Independent Clauses Joined by a Transitional Expression (*for example, therefore, furthermore, however*, etc.):**

    The oil line began to leak; however, the oil pressure remained steady. (Use a semicolon between independent clauses and a comma following the transitional expression to emphasize the break and the relationship between the clauses.)

- **Dependent Clauses Separated by a Semicolon for Clarity:**

    The cook promised to remove the parsley, tartar sauce, and pickle; toast, scrape, and butter the bun; and add lettuce, tomato, and mayonnaise.

366   Typewriter Spacing with the Semicolon

	Before	*After*
• All uses.	0	1

367   The Semicolon with Other Punctuation

- Dash, ¶ 328.

- Parentheses, ¶ 342.

- Quotation marks, ¶ 364.

UNDERSCORE OR ITALICS

368   The underscore is used by the typist as italics are used by the printer: primarily to cast special emphasis on selected expressions.

Words used as words. Underscore or italicize a word to refer to it as a word rather than for its meaning.

    Learn to replace a few <u>and</u>s and <u>but</u>s with semicolons—for variety, if for no other reason.

Note: Underscore or italicize the root word only (not the *s*). Single characters may be treated in the same manner.

> Drop the s̲ and the 5̲s in the final version.

Definitions and translations. Indicate the definition or translation of a word by underscoring or italicizing the word and enclosing the definition or translation in quotation marks.

> Laissez faire is used in economics to mean "the government does not
>   interfere with business."
> The term *laissez faire* is translated "allow (them) to do."

Individual names of vehicles. Underscore or italicize *individual* names given to vehicles.

> We read about the U̲.̲S̲.̲S̲.̲ O̲k̲l̲a̲h̲o̲m̲a̲.
> They have a Cadillac named *Strongheart*.
> The driver preferred the Mark VII tank named S̲p̲i̲t̲f̲i̲r̲e̲.

Note: Do not underscore or italicize brand names, model numbers, etc.

Titles of published works. Underscore or italicize the *exact* titles of *complete published works* (books, periodicals, plays, etc.). Use quotation marks around the titles of *sections* of such works (chapters, units, etc.). (See note below.)

> I like the chapter "Money, Credit, and Banking" in Basic Economics.

Works of art. The same rule as applied to the titles of published works may be applied to works of art: paintings, sculpture, etc.

> The statue Venus at Dawn was unveiled.

Note: As an alternative, the names of published works and works of art may be typed all in capital letters.

> I like the chapter "Money, Credit, and Banking" in BASIC
>   ECONOMICS.

Placement of underscoring. Underscore each word individually only when it is used as an individual word. Normally, underscore each *expression* as a unit.

- **As an Expression:**   Quid pro quo means "this for that."

- **As Individual Words:**   Quid, pro, and quo are Latin words.

Do not *extend* the underscore to include punctuation following the underscored material; do not *break* the underscore to skip punctuation within the underscored material.

UNIT

4

Capitalization

Using capital (uppercase) letters for emphasis is the process known as *capitalization*. We capitalize certain words to indicate their importance:

- **persons, places, or things:** *Henry Ford High* is a large school.
  Jose Sardon was chosen as an award winner.

- **first words in a sentence:** *Come* into the house immediately!

The following capitalization guidelines illustrate general areas of agreement. You should know, however, that capitalization is partly a matter of habit, so practices will vary in some businesses. Always use the capitalization preferred by your employer. Avoid unnecessary capitals!

401   Academics

Courses/subject areas. Capitalize the titles of specific courses, but do not capitalize references to general academic subject areas (except languages).

- **course:** All of our students took Psychology of Career Adjustment last fall.

- **subject area:** Ying Sun wants to take a course in history.
  She also wants to study foreign languages.
  Jack is studying German.

Degrees. Academic degrees are generally not capitalized when used with the word *degree*. The degree is capitalized when used with the name of an individual.

- **with *degree*:** The woman receiving the bachelor of science degree was cheered by her family.

We offer both the associate of arts and the associate of science degrees.

- with *name*:   Vickey Sigler, Juris Doctor, is an excellent attorney.

Note: For capitalization information on abbreviations of academic degrees, please refer to Unit 5.

402   Advertising

Specific trade names of products are always capitalized; the product itself is not capitalized unless it becomes part of the brand name.

Georgina ordered a Zenith television set.
Do you like my new Mickey Mouse watch?
The dean loves to use Heinz Catsup on scrambled eggs. (Catsup is part of the brand name.)

403   Beginning Words

Capitalize the first word of:

- **sentences:**   Our new house is north of where we live now.

- **expressions used
  as sentences:**   So what? Terrific! You're kidding! Really?

- **questions:**   Do you want to go to the show with us?

- **a complete passage
  or sentence with
  independent meaning
  following a colon:**   They agreed on one issue: The public wants higher quality products!

- **each item in a
  list or outline:**
  I. Organizing my desk
     A. Supplies
        1. Bond paper
        2. Carbon paper
        3. Onionskin paper
        4. Envelopes

- **each line of a poem:**   Come tell me of your sadness
  Where the forest flowers grow
       Where the whispering breeze
       Binds the lips of trees
  And only I will know!
                                                    —James Kavanaugh

- **quoted sentences:**   Russ told Jose, "Tonight we celebrate!"

Note: For capitalization after an opening parenthesis, see ¶ 342. For more about capitalization after a colon, see ¶ 314.

404   Celestial Bodies

Capitalize the names of planets, stars, and constellations. Do not capitalize the words *sun, moon,* or *earth* unless they are used together with the capitalized names of other celestial bodies.

> Remember the first moonwalk?
> The night was bright. We picked out the North Star and the Big Dipper.
> Scientists can predict and compare the orbits of Venus and Earth.

405   Compass Directions

Compass directions are capitalized when they refer to *specific* regions, or when the direction is part of a specific name. These words are not capitalized, however, when they merely indicate a general location or direction.

- **specific region:**   We have made reservations for our vacation in the Far East.
  Sales in our Northern Region have doubled this year.
  I was born and raised in the Middle West.

- **part of
specific name:**   The Southern Bell Telephone Company serves our state.
  Our flight was booked on Eastern Airlines Flight 402.
  Sabrina Decky is the head of the South Florida Detective Bureau.

- **general direction:**   Come north on I-95 and then west on Ives Dairy Road.
  Most of our students live on the east side of town.

Always capitalize the words *Northerner, Southerner, Easterner, Westerner,* and *Midwesterner.*

> The Easterner adapted quickly to customs in Europe.

Words such as *northern, southern, eastern,* and *western* are capitalized when they refer to people in a specific region and to their political, social, and cultural activities. They are not capitalized, however, when they merely indicate a general location or region.

Eastern merchants	Southern hospitality
the Western vote	

But: the eastern portion   westerly winds
a southern summer

406   Government

Officials and titles. Titles of international, national, and state government officials are capitalized when written before, following, or in place of a specific individual's name. These titles are not capitalized, however, when used to refer to an entire class of officials.

Ambassador   Prime Minister
Attorney General   Prince
Chief Justice   Princess
Chief of Staff   Queen
Governor   Secretary-General of the
King   United Nations
Lieutenant Governor   Secretary of State
Premier   Vice-President
President

The Ambassador from Liberia called for the vote.
Carrie Meek, State Representative, called me today.
President Roosevelt was the only individual ever elected for more than
    two terms.
Candidates for president must appeal to all voters.

Government bodies. Capitalize the names of countries and international organizations, as well as national, state, county, city, and local bodies and the agencies within them.

the United Nations   France
Department of Labor   Warren Consolidated Schools
the Cabinet   the Colorado Legislature
the Truman Administration

Short forms. Capitalize the short forms of international and national bodies and their major divisions.

the House (House of Representatives)
the Court (United States Supreme Court)
the Department (Department of Labor)
the Bureau (Federal Bureau of Investigation)
the Agency (Central Intelligence Agency)

Usually, however, do not capitalize short forms of state or local government bodies except for special emphasis.

the city (Kansas City, MO)
the board (State Board of Education)

Acts, bills, laws, treaties. Capitalize the titles of acts, bills, laws, and treaties, but do not capitalize the short form used in place of the full name.

Note: Observe the illustrated exception.

Full Title	*Short Form*
Safety Appliance Act	the act
House Bill 736	the bill

	Full Title	*Short Form*
	Public Law 94-553	the law
	the Panama Canal Treaty	the treaty
	the Constitution of the	
	United States	**But:** the Constitution

407   Hyphenated Words

Capitalize only the parts of hyphenated words that you would normally capitalize if the word were alone.

We saved a lot of money at the mid-January sale.
President-elect Adams spoke to the visitors.
The ninety-eighth Congress came to an end later than expected.
Spanish-speaking friends are helping me learn Spanish.

Beginning a sentence. When the hyphenated word begins a sentence, however, the first word is capitalized. All other words follow the previous illustrations above.

Up-to-date records are a must in this business.
One-eighth of the country's population is illiterate.
Mid-January sales this year are not attracting many buyers.

As a title. When a hyphenated word serves as a title, all parts of the hyphenated word are capitalized except articles (*the, a, an*), short prepositions (prepositions with four or fewer letters), and short conjunctions (*and, as, but, or, nor*).

Up-to-Date Grant Manual   Ninety-Eighth Congress
Mid-January Sale   Spanish-Speaking Officials
President-Elect Adams

408   Institutions

Capitalize the names of all institutions, such as churches, libraries, schools, hospitals, synagogues, colleges, and universities. Division names within a college or university are also capitalized.

Highland Park Baptist Church   Michigan State University
Detroit Public Library   College of Medicine
Del Campo High School   Business Studies Division
Variety Childrens Hospital   School of Architecture
Temple Beth Sholom   Department of Psychology
Miami-Dade Community College

409   Legal Terminology

Capitalize the important words in legal citations.

Alliance Assurance Co. v. United States
People v. Gonzalez, 35 N.Y. 49, 61-62 (1866)

In law documents, many introductory words are typed all in capital letters.

> SUBSCRIBED AND SWORN TO before me this . . .
> . . . hereinafter called the BUYER . . .
> IN WITNESS WHEREOF, the parties . . .
> THEREFORE, BE IT RESOLVED, that the . . .

410   Literary and Artistic Works

Capitalize the principal words in titles of publications (books, magazines, pamphlets, and newspapers) and other artistic works (movies, plays, songs, paintings, sculptures, and poems). Remember not to capitalize articles, short prepositions, or conjunctions unless they are the first word in the title (See ¶ 412).

Titles of complete literary and artistic works. Titles of complete published works, such as books, magazines, pamphlets, newspapers, and plays are underscored, italicized, or typed all in capital letters. Also underscored, italicized, or typed all in capitals are the titles of motion pictures, long musical compositions (symphonies, operas, etc.), paintings, sculptures, and other *complete* works of art. The titles of poems, songs, and television or radio programs are enclosed in quotation marks.

- **book:**   I found English the Easy Way very helpful in reviewing grammar rules.
               I found ENGLISH THE EASY WAY very helpful in reviewing grammar rules.
               Loretha has read *Gone with the Wind* four times.
               Loretha has read GONE WITH THE WIND four times.

- **magazine:** For her birthday, Louise received a subscription to People magazine.
               For her birthday, Louise received a subscription to PEOPLE magazine.

- **newspaper:** Every morning the *San Francisco Chronicle* is delivered before 8 o'clock.
               Every morning the SAN FRANCISCO CHRONICLE is delivered before 8 o'clock.

- **movie:**   The Sound of Music is one of the film classics being presented at the festival.
               THE SOUND OF MUSIC is one of the film classics being presented at the festival.

- **play:**   We were very moved by *The Shadow Box*, a play about dealing with death.
               We were very moved by THE SHADOW BOX, a play about dealing with death.

- **painting:** Andrew Wyeth painted *Christina's World*.
               Andrew Wyeth painted CHRISTINA'S WORLD.

- **sculpture:**   They exhibited the statue <u>Venus at Dawn</u>.
  They exhibited the statue VENUS AT DAWN.

- **song:**   Helen Reddy's "I Am Woman" speaks out for women's rights.

Portions of literary works. Chapters or subdivisions of books, magazines, pamphlets, or newspapers are enclosed in quotation marks.

- **chapter of a book:**   Please study "The Secretary and Word Processing" in the book SECRETARIAL OFFICE PROCEDURES.

- **newspaper column:**   Did you see "Action Line" in today's *Chicago Tribune*?

411   Names of Individuals

Capitalize, spell, and space the names of individuals exactly as the person does. Names containing prefixes such as *d', da, de, del, della, di, du, l', la, le, mac, mc, o', van,* and *von* vary in their capitalization and spacing. Once again, always follow individual preferences.

Jan Von Hagen	Bennie von Der Halben
William A. Stokes	Peter J. Masiko, Jr.
Maria Elena Diaz	Lina Cuan
D. J. Van Camp	Joel VanCamp

When a surname with an uncapitalized prefix is used without the first name within a sentence, capitalize the prefix to indicate immediately to the reader that it is a surname.

The only person from your department at the meeting was Christina del Campo.
The only person from your department at the meeting was Del Campo.

412   Names of Places, Things, and Ideas

Capitalize the entire titles of specific places, things, and ideas, but do not capitalize the short forms used in place of the full name.

Woodward Avenue	the avenue
Golden Gate Bridge	the bridge
Equal Rights Amendment	the amendment
Tampa Airport	the airport
the Grand Canyon	the canyon
the Penobscot Building	the building
the Statue of Liberty	the statue

When capitalizing several words in a title, do not capitalize articles (*the, a, an*), short prepositions (prepositions with four or fewer letters), or short conjunctions (*and, as, but, or, nor*).

When these words begin the title, however, they are capitalized.

Note: The definite article *the* is capitalized only when it is part of the official name.

> We have a subscription to *The Denver Post.*
> (*The* is part of the official name of the newspaper.)

But: Last summer we visited the Grand Canyon.
> (*The* is not part of the official name.)

Caution about derivatives of proper nouns. Do not capitalize some words derived from proper nouns that have developed special meanings:

bohemian	italicize
china	pasteurize
boycott	anglicize
plaster of paris	venetian blind

413   Nouns with Numbers and Letters

Nouns followed by numbers or letters should be capitalized, with the exception of the nouns *line, note, page, size,* and *verse.* The noun *paragraph* may be either capitalized or lowercased.

Appendix B	line 17
Article 4	page 203
Bulletin 129	size 7
Chapter V	note 4
Column 1	verse 2
Diagram 8	Paragraph 3
Exhibit C	paragraph 5
Figure 4	
Invoice 34-161	
Lesson 14	
Model A16	
Room 303	

414   Organizations

Capitalize the names of associations, companies, independent committees and boards, political parties, conventions, fraternities and sororities, clubs, etc. Remember to follow the individual preference indicated by the organization with regard to capitalization, spelling, and spacing. A good reference for an organization's preference is the official letterhead.

> The Sardon Furniture Company
> National Association for the Advancement
>   of Colored People
> Dean Selection and Search Committee
> Democratic National Committee

the Republican National Convention
Kappa Delta Sorority
California Club

415   Programs, Movements, and Concepts

Capitalize the specific names of programs, movements, and concepts, but do not capitalize these words when they are used as general terms.

Specific Name	*General Term*
the Communist Party	communism
Social Security Administration	social security check
Civil Rights Act	the civil rights leader

416   Race, Religion, Nationality, Language

Capitalize the names of races, religions, nationalities, tribes, peoples, and languages.

Asian	Hispanic	Judaism	French	Afro-American
Anglo	Baptist	Spanish	Catholic	English

Supreme beings. Capitalize all references to a supreme being.

Jesus Christ	Buddha	Mohammed	the Messiah
Holy Spirit	God	Yahweh	

Capitalize personal pronouns referring to a supreme being when they stand alone, but do not capitalize them when the pronoun is preceded by an antecedent.

We ask *His* blessing on this food.
But: We ask the Lord for *his* blessing.

417   Relatives

Titles of relatives are capitalized when they precede a name, or when the title itself is used as a name. Such family titles, however, are not capitalized when they are preceded by possessive pronouns and/or when they simply describe a family relationship.

Mom and Dad sent me a check for my birthday.
He went to pick up Uncle Ken.
I want Aunt Leota and Aunt Sammy to visit our new house.
Grandpa, can you fix this for me?
Can Grandma paint a picture for my room, too?

But: My aunt and uncle have been married 20 years.
I would like you to meet my cousin Barbara. (describing relationship)

418   Time

Capitalize the names of days and months.

- **days/months:**   December   January   October
                      Monday   Wednesday   Saturday

Capitalize the names of holidays and religious days.

- **holidays/**   Passover   Yom Kipper   Semana Santa
  religious days: Mother's Day Halloween   New Year's Eve

Capitalize the names of historical events and nicknames used for historical periods.

- **historical**   World War I   the Great Depression
  events: the Civil War   the Depression

Do not capitalize the names of decades and centuries unless they are part of a nickname.

- **decades/**   in the forties   during the nineteenth
  centuries: in the nineteen-eighties   century

         But: the Roaring Twenties

Seasons of the year are not capitalized unless they are part of a specific title or are personified.

- **seasons:**   spring fever   winter winds   fall colors

         But: Spring/Summer Term
                  Spring Clearance Sale
                  Oh Wicked Winter, are you with us forever?

419   Titles

Official titles preceding names. Capitalize all formal titles when they precede personal names.

Mr. Bill Watson   Governor-elect Julio Avello
Mrs. Joycelyn Simon   ex-Senator Graham
Ms. Barbara Gray   Rabbi Silverstein
Vice-President Hernandez   Reverend Kenneth Long
Secretary Rod Forrest   Ambassador Diana Wiggins
Dr. Lu Sheng   Judge Ellen Morphonios
Professor Beverly Creely   Representative Carrie Meek

Do not capitalize such titles when the personal name that follows is set off by commas as an appositive.

         The vice-president, Roberto Hernandez, will arrive tonight.
But: Vice-President Roberto Hernandez will arrive tonight.

Occupational titles. Do not capitalize occupational titles when they precede or follow personal names.

The introduction was made by surgeon Marie Hernandez-Fumero.
We had dinner at the home of John Williams, attorney.

But: When the occupational title is a specific job title:

Senior Editor Adam Walters is working with me on my book.

Official titles following names. Generally, do not capitalize official titles when they follow a personal name or are used in place of a personal name.

Note: Exceptions are made for high governmental titles; see ¶ 406.

Dr. Carol Zion, president of Cornell University, will speak to-night.

Roberto Hernandez, vice-president, will sign the certificate.

Some companies capitalize some or all titles of company officials. Always follow the practices used by your employer in such cases and respect the preferences of others regarding their own names and titles.

Academic titles for the doctorate degree. With academic titles for the doctorate degree, use *Dr.* before the name *or* the academic abbreviation following the name.

Dr. Alan Eisenberg   *or*   Alan Eisenberg, Ph.D.

Incorrect: Dr. Alan Eisenberg, Ph.D.

420   Within Business Letters

Capitalize the first word in a business letter salutation or complimentary close.

Salutation	*Complimentary Close*
Dear Mr. Swanson	Sincerely
My dear Dr. Stokes	Very truly yours
Ladies and Gentlemen	Sincerely yours

Capitalize the first letter in the headings *Attention* and *Subject*. (*Subject* may also be typed all in capital letters.)

Attention Wanda Blake
Subject: Office Procedures
SUBJECT: Office Procedures

Note: For more information on typing business letters, please refer to Unit 10.

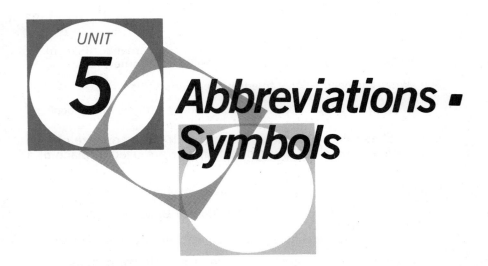

5 *Abbreviations ▪ Symbols*

When there is a need to save both space and time in writing, words are often shortened. These shortened words are known as *abbreviations*. There are some abbreviations that everyone uses:

Mr. Harry Hoffman	instead of	*Mister* Harry Hoffman
Mrs. Beverly Williams	instead of	*Mistress* Beverly Williams

Others are unique to certain occupations.

5

501   Basic Rules

Cautious use. While the use of abbreviations saves both time and space, be careful to use only those abbreviations that readers will recognize. Check with your dictionary or other reference for acceptable forms of abbreviations not listed in this section.

Consistency. Be consistent! You will find that many abbreviations are used with and without spaces and periods. While both versions of an abbreviation may be acceptable, using both versions within the same letter or report is *not* acceptable. Once you use one form of an abbreviation, use the same form throughout.

Spacing and punctuation.

- **Single words:** Use period at end   Dr. Ms. Inc.
    But: Shortened words   memo photo 4th

- **All capitals:** No periods, no spaces   IBM   YMCA/YWCA
    But: Academic degrees   B.S. M.A. A.S.
            Geographic   U.S.A. U.S.S.R.
                                    (See ¶ 507.)
            Other exceptions   A.D. B.C.

- **All lowercase:**   Use periods, no spaces   a.m. e.g. p.m.
- **Two or more words:** Use periods and spaces   loc. cit.   Lt. Col.
  But: Academic degrees   Ed.D.   Ph.D.   M.Ed.
                         Measurements   sq m   cu cm

502   Academic Degrees

Academic degrees are generally written with periods, but no spaces.

Bachelor of Arts	B.A.
Doctor of Education	Ed.D.

503   Broadcasting Stations

Radio and television stations are assigned call letters. The call letters are written in capitals with no periods or spaces:

WIOD   ABC   UPI News Service   KOA

504   Business Abbreviations

Many business and professional organizations are known by abbreviated names. Generally, these abbreviated names are typed in capital letters with no periods and no spaces.

IBM   AFL-CIO   YMCA/YWCA   NOW   PTA

505   Data Processing

Rapidly growing data processing terminology is frequently written using abbreviations: FORTRAN, COBOL, OCR.

506   Foreign Expressions

Common foreign expressions are frequently abbreviated: e.g.—*exempli gratia* (for example); etc.—*et cetera* (and so forth); i.e.—*id est* (that is).

507   Geographic Abbreviations

Geographic abbreviations are generally written in capital letters with periods, but no spaces. The periods are also omitted occasionally:

U.S.A. (USA)   U.S.S.R. (USSR)

Names of states, districts, and territories of the United States have frequently used abbreviations. The postal ZIP (Zone Improvement Program) two-letter state codes are also commonly used abbreviations. Remember to be consistent in the use of these and other abbreviations. Table 5-1 lists the names, abbreviations, and capitals of the states, districts, and territories of the United States. Table 5-2 lists the names, abbreviations, and capitals of the Canadian provinces.

508   Government Agencies

Abbreviations for government agencies are generally written in capital letters with no periods and no spaces:

CIA   NASA   AEC   FHA   FICA

509   Measurements

Units of measurement are abbreviated when they appear frequently, as in invoices and other business forms, tables, and scientific works. These units of measure are now commonly used without periods:

15 lb 3 oz   4 ft 6 in

510   Personal Names and Initials

Frequently, personal names are shortened. When using such abbreviations, use a period at the end and space once after the period before typing the last name:

Chas. Johnson (Charles)   Robt. O'Henry (Robert)
Geo. Weber (George)   Thos. McFarland (Thomas)
Jas. Clayborne (James)   Wm. Michelson (William)

Some shortened names become accepted nicknames and are not followed by a period:

Kathie (Katherine)   Bev (Beverly)
Chris (Christine)   Joe (Joseph)

When using initials in place of a name, or in addition to another name, space once after each period following an initial:

M. Duane Hansen   Russell K. Sigler
D. M. Macksoud

Be sure to follow an individual's personal preference in using abbreviated names, nicknames, or initials.

511   Personal Titles

A personal title is abbreviated when written before a full name:

Mr. Rick Gettings   Dr. Barbara Gray
Ms. Joycelyn Simon   Mrs. Alina Hernandez-Fumero

TABLE 5-1

State, District, and Territory Names; Abbreviations; Capitals

The following table shows the names of the states, districts, and territories of the United States; the standard abbreviations of the names; the two-letter abbreviations that are used with ZIP Codes; and the capital cities.

Name	Standard Abbreviation	Two-Letter Abbreviation	Capital
Alabama	Ala.	AL	Montgomery
Alaska	Alaska	AK	Juneau
Arizona	Ariz.	AZ	Phoenix
Arkansas	Ark.	AR	Little Rock
California	Calif.	CA	Sacramento
Colorado	Colo.	CO	Denver
Connecticut	Conn.	CT	Hartford
Delaware	Del.	DE	Dover
District of Columbia	D.C.	DC	Washington (National capital)
Florida	Fla.	FL	Tallahassee
Georgia	Ga.	GA	Atlanta
Guam	Guam	GU	Agana
Hawaii	Hawaii	HI	Honolulu
Idaho	Idaho	ID	Boise
Illinois	Ill.	IL	Springfield
Indiana	Ind.	IN	Indianapolis
Iowa	Iowa	IA	Des Moines
Kansas	Kans.	KS	Topeka
Kentucky	Ky.	KY	Frankfort
Louisiana	La.	LA	Baton Rouge
Maine	Maine	ME	Augusta
Maryland	Md.	MD	Annapolis
Massachusetts	Mass.	MA	Boston
Michigan	Mich.	MI	Lansing
Minnesota	Minn.	MN	St. Paul
Mississippi	Miss.	MS	Jackson
Missouri	Mo.	MO	Jefferson City
Montana	Mont.	MT	Helena
Nebraska	Nebr.	NE	Lincoln
Nevada	Nev.	NV	Carson City
New Hampshire	N. H.	NH	Concord
New Jersey	N. J.	NJ	Trenton
New Mexico	N. Mex.	NM	Santa Fe
New York	N. Y.	NY	Albany

(continued)

TABLE 5-1 *(continued)*

Name	Standard Abbreviation	Two-Letter Abbreviation	Capital
North Carolina	N. C.	NC	Raleigh
North Dakota	N. Dak.	ND	Bismarck
Ohio	Ohio	OH	Columbus
Oklahoma	Okla.	OK	Oklahoma City
Oregon	Oreg.	OR	Salem
Pennsylvania	Pa.	PA	Harrisburg
Puerto Rico	P. R.	PR	San Juan
Rhode Island	R. I.	RI	Providence
South Carolina	S. C.	SC	Columbia
South Dakota	S. Dak.	SD	Pierre
Tennessee	Tenn.	TN	Nashville
Texas	Tex.	TX	Austin
Utah	Utah	UT	Salt Lake City
Vermont	Vt.	VT	Montpelier
Virgin Islands	V. I.	VI	Charlotte Amalie
Virginia	Va.	VA	Richmond
Washington	Wash.	WA	Olympia
West Virginia	W. Va.	WV	Charleston
Wisconsin	Wis.	WI	Madison
Wyoming	Wyo.	WY	Cheyenne

TABLE 5-2

Canadian Names, Abbreviations, and Capitals

The following table shows the names of the Canadian provinces, the standard abbreviations of the names, the two-letter abbreviations of the names, and the capitals of the provinces.

Name	Standard Abbreviation	Two-Letter Abbreviation	Capital
Alberta	Alta.	AB	Edmonton
British Columbia	B.C.	BC	Victoria
Manitoba	Man.	MB	Winnipeg
New Brunswick	N.B.	NB	Fredericton
Newfoundland	Newf./Nfld.	NF	St. John's
Northwest Territories	N.W. Ter.	NT	Yellowknife
Nova Scotia	N.S.	NS	Halifax
Ontario	Ont.	ON	Toronto
Prince Edward Island	P.E.I.	PE	Charlottetown
Quebec	Que.	PQ	Quebec
Saskatchewan	Sask.	SK	Regina
Yukon Territory		YT	Whitehorse

Note: An exception is made in the case of the title *Reverend*. *The*, as an article preceding the title *Reverend*, is the conservative usage, although the growing practice in America (as distinguished from that in England) is to use the title *Reverend* alone. When preceded by *the*, the title *Reverend* is *not* abbreviated.

Reverend James Ward   the Reverend James Ward
Rev. James Ward

With the exception of *Dr., Mr., Mrs., Ms., Messrs.,* and *Mmes.,* personal titles are generally written in full when preceding the last name only.

Professor Gertner   Judge Fuller

512   Time

Days and months. Days of the week and months of the year should not be abbreviated, except in tables where space is extremely limited.

Clock hours. Use the lowercase *a.m.* and *p.m.* with expressions of time:

We arrived today at 8:15 a.m.

513   Symbols

Symbols are another form of abbreviations. They reduce the time and space necessary to communicate information. Commonly used business and mathematical symbols are given on page 100. For common proofreader's symbols, see Unit 9, ¶ 912.

BUSINESS SYMBOLS

Symbol	Definition	Example
´	accent	Buenos días
&	ampersand (*and* sign)	Kaufey & Miller
*	asterisk	*Note
@	at, each	@ $14
{ }	braces	Nancy Mohammed } 5:00 p.m. Juan
[ ]	brackets	[Example B]
H_2O	chemistry symbols	CO_2 (Use variable line spacer.)
¢	cents	15¢
©	copyright	© South-Western Publishing Co.
°	degree, degrees	88°
/	diagonal	and/or, either/or, 3/4
$	dollar, dollars	$18
12^2	exponent	10^5 (Use variable line spacer.)
'	feet; minutes	6'
"	inches	18"
:	is to; ratio	4:3
#	number (before figure)	#943
¶	paragraph sign	new ¶
%	percent	100%
#	pound (after figure)	16#
R	registered	R. (® or R U.S. Patent Office)
§	section	US § 1441
/S/	signed (before copied signature)	/S/ *John Smith* (diagonal, S, diagonal)

MATHEMATICAL SYMBOLS

+	plus	4 + 4
−	minus	8 − 3
±	plus or minus	±5
× or •	multiplied by	10 × 10; 11 • 11
÷	divided by	14 ÷ 2
=	equal to	5 × 5 = 25
≠	not equal to	3 ≠ 5 + 1
>	greater than	15 > 5
<	less than	5 < 15

UNIT 6
Word Division

601   Some writers employ a single extreme rule for word division: *Don't*. At the other extreme, some go to great lengths to keep the right margin straight. The conventions described here represent the middle ground. Most writers employ these or similar criteria to bring a reasonably attractive balance to their work and to make reading easier. See ¶ 1305 for reference material on word division, including word lists indicating correct division.

Note: In the following illustrations, both the diagonal (/) and the dot indicate word division. The diagonal indicates points at which division is *recommended*. The dot indicates points at which division is *acceptable*, but *not preferred*.

Syllables. Divide words between syllables.

lei/sure	con•sti/tute	length/wise	mea/sure
far/ther	fol/lowed	moun/tain	im•por/tant

602   **Short Words**

Words of five or fewer letters. Do not divide words of five (or fewer than five) letters.

easy   among   space   apple

Six-letter words. *Avoid* dividing words of six letters.

awakes   bidder   finger   lately

One-syllable words. Do not divide one-syllable words.

helped   eighth   spoiled   drowned

603　　**Rules for Dividing Words in Typewritten Material**

- Divide no more than three or four words on each page you type. The key to accomplishing this is establishing the exact location of the right margin *before* typing. It is easy to allow the right margin to creep to the right or left as the page is typed.

- Avoid dividing words at the ends of the first and last lines of a paragraph.

- Avoid dividing words at the ends of the first and last lines on a page.

- Avoid creating a mental image that must be corrected when the second part of the word is read. (*car-mine, gun-wales, her-alds, his-tory*).

- The first part of the divided word must contain at least two letters; the latter part must contain at least three.

around (not a-round)　　elapsed (not e-lapsed)　　lately (not late-ly)
marker (not mark-er)　　teacher (not teach-er)　　friendly (not friend-ly)
press/ing　　　　　　　teach/ing　　　　　　　con/form
re·lated　　　　　　　　ad·heres

Note: Leaving a two-letter syllable at the beginning of a word is acceptable, but not recommended.

604　　**Single-Letter Syllables**

If a single-letter syllable falls within a word, type that syllable with the first part of the word.

reg u/late = regu/late　　　　cre a/tion = crea/tion
ma·nip u/late = ma·nipu/late　　gas o/line = gaso/line

Note 1: An exception to this rule occurs when a single-vowel syllable immediately precedes an ending two-letter syllable. In this case, both syllables should be carried over to the next line.

read/ily　　　stead/ily

Note 2: A second exception to this rule occurs when the single-letter syllable *a* or *i* is followed by the ending syllable *ble, bly, cle,* or *cal*. In this case, both syllables should be carried over to the next line.

laud/able　　mir/acle　　cler/ical　　fa·vor/ably

Two single-letter syllables. If 2 one-letter syllables occur together within a word, divide between the one-letter syllables.

anx i/e ty = anxi/ety　　con·tin u/a tion = con·tinu/ation

605   Doubled Consonants

When a root word:

- Ends in *vowel-consonant*, and
- The final consonant is doubled to add a suffix,
- *Divide between the doubled consonants.*

transm<u>it</u>	b<u>id</u>
transmit/ter	bid/ding

When a root word ends with a doubled consonant, divide between the root word and the suffix.

call/ing   stuff/ing

606   Letter *L*

When the letter *l* is:

- Pronounced with a liquid sound (as in *dwindle* or *sizzle*)
- Found immediately preceding a suffix

dwindle (ing)   sizzle (ing)

- *Carry over one or more consonants, dividing between syllables.*

dwind/ling   siz/zling

607   Suffixes

Some suffixes are always *treated* as single syllables for purposes of word division—even when additional letters (or syllables) are added. The most common of these are shown below; some of the possible additional letters and syllables are shown also. See ¶¶ 604 and 605.

cant	fied	ibly	late(ly)
cent	fier	ical(ly)	ment(s)
cial(ly)	geous(ly)	icle(s)	sial(s)
cious(ly)	ible(s)	ing(ly) (s)	sine

sion(al) (ed) (s)	tion (al) (ed)
sive(ly)	(ing) (s)
ship(s)	tious(ly)
tial(s)	tive(ly)

608   Compound Words

Hyphenated compound words. Divide hyphenated compound words at existing hyphens only.

brother-/in-/law   one-/half

Note: See ¶ 335 on writing compound words.

Solid compound words. Divide written-solid compound words between the elements of the compound word.

| checkbook | headache | bookkeepers |
| check/book | head/ache | book/keep•ers |

Note: If overall appearance is improved, divide elsewhere, as in *book-keepers*, above. See ¶ 335 on writing compound words.

609   Dates, Proper Names, Addresses

It it is necessary to divide a date, a proper name, or an address, maximize readability and appearance.

April 18,/1775	Between the day and the year.
Ms. Cynthia/Murdock	Not between Ms. and the name.
Richard/Adams, M.D.	Not between the name and the degree.
Chicago,/IL 60616	Preferably, between city and state.

610   Figures, Abbreviations, Symbols

Avoid dividing between figures, abbreviations, and symbols.

$15,000	Not: $15/000
P & G	Not: P/& G; Not: P &/G
#231	Not: #/231; Not: #2/31, etc.

611   Contractions

Do not divide contractions.

couldn't   isn't   they're   you'll

UNIT 7 *Numbers*

There are *three* widely used styles of writing numbers:

- *Formal style,* in which most (almost all) numbers are written in words. Formal style is used to convey an image of formal elegance.

Formal

Half Past the Hour
of
Seven
In the Evening

- *Technical style,* in which most (almost all) numbers are written in figures. A simple table of technical data would be nearly impossible to express in formal style.

CURRENT REQUIREMENTS

Point	Volts	Amps
A	115	3
B	115	15
C	240	30

- *General style,* in which words are used to achieve formality when formality is appropriate, and figures are used to achieve clarity and efficiency of organization when clarity and efficiency are more important than formality.

General style is found in most newspapers, magazines, and business correspondence—any writing in which the emphasis is neither clearly on the formal nor clearly on the technical.

In business correspondence (general style), a formal invitation to an important conference may merit the same formality accorded the mayor's proclamation. On the other hand, the next piece of business correspondence typed by the same person may require the clarity of a data table.

In this chapter, all conventions and examples pertain to general style unless formal style or technical style is specified.

GENERAL CONVENTIONS

701   Small Numbers

Small numbers in formal style. Write the numbers 1-100 in words; larger numbers in figures.

> Whereas this is the thirty-seventh year of . . .
> The price is modest: Seventy-five dollars.

Exception: In *very* formal writing, longer numbers are sometimes written in words.

> . . . Seventeen Hundred and Seventy-Six

Note: See ¶ 732 on writing numbers in words.

Small numbers in technical style. In technical style, express all numbers in figures, regardless of their size.

> 2 tbs. salt   3 cups sugar   2 amperes   4 ft   8 ohms

Small numbers in general style. Write the numbers 1-10 in words; larger numbers in figures. See ¶ 703 for sentences containing more than one number.

> Send five cases next week.
> Send 25 cases next week.

702   Round Numbers

Round numbers in formal style. In formal style, spell out all round numbers that can be written in one or two words.

> twenty thousand   three hundred
> thirty-two million   (*Thirty-two* is a single compound word.)

Round numbers in technical style. In technical style, express all numbers in figures.

> 27,000   300   32,000,000 32×10^6

Note: Scientific notation is frequently used in technical writing to express large round numbers.

$$10^2 = 100 \qquad 10^5 = 100,000$$
$$10^3 = 1000 \qquad 10^6 = 1,000,000$$
$$10^4 = 10,000 \qquad 10^7 = 10,000,000$$
$$2.75 \times 10^6 = 2,750,000$$

Round numbers in general style. If the intent is smoothness in sentence structure, use *formal style*, spelling out round numbers that can be expressed in one or two words.

> five hundred   six thousand   seventy-three thousand

Note: *Seventy-three* is a single compound word.

If the intent is clarity—to emphasize the numbers—write round numbers in figures, as you would in *technical style*.

> 500   6000 or 6,000   73,000

When writing for either formality or clarity, round numbers 1,000,000 and more may be written using figures and words *combined*:

> 25 million   120 billion $17 million
> 24.75 million   119½ billion $ 2.4 trillion

Note: Hyphenate spelled-out numbers from twenty-one through ninety-nine, even when they are part of a larger number.

> twenty-six   two hundred thirty-seven

703   Consistency

Use the same form (figures, words, or combined figures and words) within each *set* of numbers. *Sets* of numbers are those related to one another for a variety of reasons.

Numbers in a category. Numbers in the same category may be considered a set, even if they are widely separated in a book, magazine article, etc.

> Nine typists participated in the contest. One (the fastest) typed 92 w.p.m. Another (the slowest) typed 8 w.p.m. All nine had some formal instruction in typing.

Some writers use words and figures to keep categories separate when the occasion permits. In the paragraph above, the number of typists is expressed in words; their typing speeds are expressed in figures.

Numbers in the same sentence or paragraph. It may be desirable, in technical style or general style, to treat the numbers in a sentence or paragraph as a single set simply because they fall within the same sentence or paragraph.

> All 9 typists participated in the contest. The fastest participant typed 92 w.p.m. The slowest typed 8 w.p.m. All 9 had some formal instruction in typing.

Note: Convert from *words* to *figures* to achieve consistency, except in formal writing or when that conversion causes a sentence to begin with a figure. If the sentence would begin with a figure, it is preferable to spell out the number, even though figures are used later in the sentence.

Not: 7 workers used a total of 38 tools.

But: Seven workers used a total of 38 tools.

Or: The 7 workers used a total of 38 tools.

Consistency in formal style. In formal style, the conversion to achieve consistency should be from figures to words, when feasible.

Not: The seminar will be held at 1327 Third Avenue South.

Nor: The seminar will be held at 1327 3d Avenue South.

But: The seminar will be held at thirteen twenty-seven Third Avenue South.

RANGES

704 **General style.** Use a hyphen between the high and low numbers when indicating a range.

General and Technical: The range of their ages is 5-12.
(The actual ages are: 5, 6, 6, 7, 11, 11, and 12.)

Formal: Their ages range from five through twelve.

Selected numbers. If *selected* numbers are identified, separate them with commas.

> Study questions 97, 107, and 112.

Abbreviating numbers in a range. The higher number in a range may be abbreviated if:

• Both numbers have at least three digits.

• Neither number ends in 00.

To abbreviate, use the *changed* part of the higher number only.

100-107	100-107	1007-1009	1007-9
107-109	107-9	127-148	127-48
1000-1007	1000-1007	1327-1348	1327-48

Note: It is clearer to write both numbers in full than to change more than two numbers:

1327-1448 is clearer than 1327-448.

ADJACENT NUMBERS

705   **Adjacent numbers stated similarly.** When adjacent numbers are both in words or both in figures, use a comma to separate them.

> On truck 417, 12 cases are missing.
> If you have five, six would be even better.

Adjacent numbers and compound words. When one of two adjacent numbers is part of a compound word used as a modifier, spell out the smaller number and write the larger in figures.

> 27 four-pronged forks   two 4-pronged forks
> 75 ten-dollar bills   seven 10-dollar bills

ADDRESSES

706   **House numbers.** House or building numbers are usually written in figures before the name on the street. However, when the number *one* (1) is used alone, it is spelled out. All other single-digit house or building numbers are written as figures.

> One Marina Avenue   115 N. E. Eighth Street   4309 Huntington Avenue

Formal addresses. Some persons write their addresses more formally, using *words* rather than *figures*. It is considered courteous to address all persons and organizations as they identify *themselves*.

> Two Page Road   Six Thousand Gulfshore Boulevard

Street numbers. The numbers of streets (for those streets assigned *numbers* instead of *names*) are usually spelled out if they are ten or smaller; written in figures if they are larger than ten. In order to avoid confusion, use a hyphen preceded and followed by a space when figures are used for both the house number and the street name.

> 122 Fifth Avenue South   2447 - 43d Street

Highways. State, interstate, and federal highways are identified with figures.

S.R. 863   I-75   U.S. 41

Note: In the interstate system:

- (I-70)   Two-digit even numbers generally run east and west.

- (I-95)   Two-digit odd numbers generally run north and south.

- (I-480) Three-digit even numbers are connectors running *through* major cities.

- (I-275) Three-digit odd numbers are connectors running *around* major cities.

ZIP Codes. Zoning Improvement Program Codes are preceded by a standard two-letter abbreviation of a state name.

1532 Sunset Boulevard   222 Georgetown Road
Los Angeles, CA   90028-1015   Jacksonville, NC   28540-2086

Note: See ¶ 1230 for nine-digit ZIP Codes.

AGE

707   Ages are usually written out, since, in *general* use, there is nothing *technical* about them.

They will celebrate their twenty-third birthdays tomorrow.

Note: When ages *are* written in figures, use *cardinal* numbers (1, 43, etc.). Use *ordinal* numbers for birthdays (1st, 3d, 29th, 398th, etc.).

Age in formal documents. In formal documents, ages are spelled out.

He is in his thirty-fourth year.
At the age of three, she behaved as an adult.

Statistics. When ages are used statistically, presented in tabular form, or otherwise processed as data, write them in figures.

Subject	Age
A	14
B	12
C	17

Age with name. When a name is followed by the person's age, the age is set off with commas.

Wilma Immokalee, twenty-three, was reported missing.
Wilma Immokalee, 23, was reported missing. (This form is not used in formal style.)

Precise age. When age is stated precisely in months, days, and years, write the age in figures.

The child is 2 years, 11 months, and 27 days old.

But: The child is three days old.
The child is seven months old.

ANNIVERSARIES

708   **General style.** Spell out the numbers necessary to identify an anniversary unless three or more words are required.

This is their twenty-fifth wedding anniversary.
This is the 227th anniversary of the event.

Formal style. In *formal* writing, spell out the numbers necessary to identify an anniversary, even if it takes several words.

This is the one hundred thirty-eighth anniversary of the founding of the organization.

DATES

709   **Dates in normal order.** Use *cardinal* numbers to express dates appearing in normal month-day-year order. *Cardinal numbers* are 1, 3, 29, 398, etc.

April 18, 1775   July 4, 1776

Not: April 18th, 1775   **Not:** July 4th, 1776

(For conventions regarding the *dateline* in business correspondence, see ¶ 1005.)

Month out of normal order or not stated. If the month follows the day, or if the month is not stated, use *ordinal numbers* (1st, 2d, 3d, etc.) or *ordinal words* (first, second, third, etc.).

General Style: The accident occurred on the 12th of May.

Formal Style: Yes, it was the eighteenth of April in seventy-five.

Technical Style: April 18, 1775.

Military and foreign dates. In the U.S. military and in certain foreign nations, dates are stated in day-month-year sequence.

24 January 1925   12 May 1950

In this format, the day is written in cardinal figures (1, 2, 12, 27, etc.), not ordinals (1st, 2d, 12th, 27th, etc.).

Formal dates. In formal documents, dates should be written in words.

> April eighteenth, seventeen hundred and seventy-five
> the eighteenth of April in the year of our Lord seventeen hundred and seventy-five

Decades and centuries. Decades and centuries should be spelled out in all styles (formal, technical, and general).

the twenty-first century   in the seventies

But: in the 1980s

B.C. and A.D. The initials *B.C.* and *A.D.* are typed after the number that identifies the year.

1203 A.D.   432 B.C.

Contracted form. Dates may be written in contracted form ('33, '55) if:

- They are of historical significance.

the '37 flood

- They are years of graduation.

the class of '44
the class of '03

- Several years of the same century are used in the same passage.

> There was a severe flood in 1937 and lesser ones in '39, '41, and '47.

DECIMALS AND FRACTIONS

710   Decimals

When a period is used as a decimal, do not leave a space before it or after it.

2.27   .007 $32.41   327

Note: It is not necessary to have a digit *before* a decimal, but there should be at least one digit *after* a decimal.

.007   327 (no decimal)

711   Fractions

A fraction should be spelled out.

two-thirds   seven-eighths   three-fourths

Unless: • It is part of a mixed number.

The length is 3 1/3 times the width.

Use the diagonal (/) for "made" fractions. Notice the space between the whole number and the fraction. If any fraction in a set of numbers is "made," all fractions in the set must be "made."

Not: The sizes are 7½ and 6 7/8.

But: The sizes are 7 1/2 and 6 7/8.

• It is used in a mathematical statement.

$$x = 3/8 \, y(z - 7)$$

• It is awkward when written in words.

Not: thirty-seven sixty-fourths

But: 37/64

Fractions in words. When a fraction is written in words, the numerator and denominator are joined by a hyphen.

seven-eighths   three-fourths   four-nineteenths

Unless: One part (the numerator or the denominator) already contains a hyphen.

Not: one-sixty-fourth   **Not:** forty-three-sixty-fourths

But: one sixty-fourth   **But:** forty-three sixty-fourths

Fractions are not ordinals. Do not use a word or suffix as part of the denominator. Avoid *of an inch* and similar constructions.

Not: 9/32ds   7/64ths   1/2 an inch   3/8ths of an inch

But: 9/32   7/64   1/2 inch   3/8 inch

Note: An *of* phrase or a similar construction may be used following a spelled-out fraction.

one-quarter of an ounce   half an hour (not 1/2 an hour)

LAW DOCUMENTS

712   **Numbers in both words and figures.** In law documents (wills, agree-
ments, etc.) and negotiable instruments (checks, certain notes,
bonds, etc.), numbers (particularly amounts of money) are stated
in words *and* figures for extra clarity and certainty.

> fifty-three dollars ($53)   seventeen (17) weeks
> One Hundred Sixty-Seven and 41/100 Dollars ($167.41)

Note: Use the word *and* no more than once in a number. If the number
consists of dollars and cents, the *and* should be used *between*
dollars and cents.

Not: Two Hundred and Five and 17/100 Dollars

But: Two Hundred Five and 17/100 Dollars

Note: Capitalization is optional—capitals as shown are preferred.

METRICS

> See ¶ 808.

MONEY

713   **General Style**

> Amounts of money are generally expressed in figures.

> $3.27 $10   nearly $20   over $5000

Indefinite money amounts. An indefinite amount of money should
be written in words unless the result is too long or awkward.

> several thousand dollars   many millions of dollars

Isolated money amount. In general style, a single isolated money
amount may be spelled out if the result is not awkward or too
lengthy.

> thirty-five dollars   three hundred dollars   five dollars

Not: three dollars and twenty-seven cents

Large money amounts. Round number amounts of $1 million and
more may be written as follows:

> $3 million $5 1/2 million $10.1 billion
> $30 million $7 3/4 million $5.83 billion

- The word (*million, billion*, etc.) must be at least *million*.

- The amount written in figures must include a whole number.

- It may, in addition, include a decimal of no more than three digits

    $7.125 million

or an equivalent fraction.

    $7 1/8 million

Not: $7.3472 million
     $7 17/49 million

714   Related Numbers

Numbers in the same set (related to one another) are written in the same manner.

Not: The $5 million building had a $500,000 tower.

But: The $5,000,000 building had a $500,000 tower.

Note: When using the *number-word* form to express a *range*, repeat the *word* to avoid confusion.

Not: $7 to $10 million ($7 or $7 million?)

But: $7 million to $10 million

715   Decimals and Zeros Following Money Amounts

When writing money amounts in figures, do not use zeros (or a decimal) after even amounts.

The amount is $352 this month. It will be $35 the first week and $17.50 each week thereafter.

But: Do keep the low-order (right) digits straight (aligned in a column) in lists and tables.

$15.75
 3.00
 7.50
$26.25

716   Cents

Generally, write amounts less than a dollar in figures and use the ¢ symbol.

35¢   17¢   97¢

Cents in formal style. In formal writing, or in stating an isolated amount in cents, spell out the amount and the word *cents*.

thirty-five cents   seventeen cents   ninety-seven cents

Cents as part of a set. If an amount is less than a dollar, but is part of a set in which some amounts are a dollar or more, use *$ .82* as the form.

The prices were $1.27, $ .82, and $3.76, respectively.

Cents in technical writing. In technical writing, use the ¢ symbol when all money amounts in a set are less than a dollar.

The price quotation increased from 82¢ to 94¢.

ORDINAL NUMBERS

717 **General style.** Spell out ordinal numbers that can be written in one or two words (counting a hyphenated word as a single word). Write other ordinals in figures, *except in formal writing*.

your twenty-third birthday   the 127th time it has happened

Ordinals in formal writing. In formal writing, spell out ordinal numbers.

the one hundred thirty-fifth anniversary of their charter

Ordinals and numerals following surnames. *Roman* numerals or ordinals written as figures may be used following surnames to designate seniority.

Raphael Azuto, 2d   Ralph Sanders III

Note: In either form, the comma is optional.

PLURALS

718 **Figures.** To form the plural of figures, add *s*.

Three 8s were printed in a row.
The 1980s are, in some respects, similar to the '20s.

Spelled-out numbers. To form the plurals of spelled-out numbers, follow the general conventions for pluralizing as illustrated below:

three   twenty-five   twenty
threes   twenty-fives   twenties
thirds   twenty-fifths   twentieths

PERCENT

719   **General style.** In general style, express percentages in figures; spell out the word *percent*.

> 17 percent   57 percent   43 percent

Note: At the beginning of a sentence, spell the number out or reword the sentence.

Not: 43 percent of those present abstained.

But: Forty-three percent of those present abstained.

Or: Among those present, 43 percent abstained.

Percent in formal writing. In formal writing, spell out the amount and the word *percent*.

> Finally, ninety-seven percent of those present voted on the issue.

Percent in technical writing. In technical writing, use the % symbol instead of the word percent.

> 17%   57%   43%

Fraction of one percent. A fraction of one percent is written:

> ½ percent   1/2 percent   .5%   0.5%

Mixed number as percent. A percentage may be expressed as a mixed number or as a decimal.

> 3½ percent   3½%   3.5 percent   3.5%   3 1/2%

RATIOS AND PROPORTIONS

720   Ratios and proportions are always written in figures.

> 5 to 1   5:2   23-57

ROMAN NUMERALS

721   Roman numerals are used most frequently to identify the major sections of an outline. They are also used (in lowercase form—xiv, etc.) to number pages in the front sections of many books. Roman numerals are also used in the title and credits sections of motion pictures, on buildings, and in other applications in which the writer or designer wishes to convey an image of historical significance.

Table 7-1 shows equivalent Roman numerals for some Arabic figures.

Table 7-1

Arabic Figures and Equivalent Roman Numerals

1	I	11	XI	30	XXX	400	CCCC
2	II	12	XII	40	XL	500	D
3	III	13	XIII	50	L	600	DC
4	IV	14	XIV	60	LX	700	DCC
5	V	15	XV	70	LXX	800	DCCC
6	VI	16	XVI	80	LXXX	900	CM
7	VII	17	XVII	90	XC	1,000	M
8	VIII	18	XVIII	100	C	2,000	MM
9	IX	19	XIX	200	CC	5,000	$\overline{V}$*
10	X	20	XX	300	CCC	10,000	$\overline{X}$*

* A line over a numeral multiplies the value by 1,000.

Other combinations of Roman numerals are built by prefixing or annexing letters. The prefixing of a letter is equivalent to subtracting the value of that letter, while the annexing is equivalent to addition.

49 is L minus X plus IX *or* XLIX.
64 is L plus X plus IV *or* LXIV.

SCORES

722   Scores of sporting events, etc., are always written in figures.

5 to 1   23-57

SYMBOLS

723   Use *figures* with symbols and abbreviations.

#3   15%   46¢ $44   142 sq ft   18 in

In a range or series of numbers, repeat symbols and abbreviations but not words.

Ranges { 17%-22%   17 through 22 percent
         { $25-$27   twenty-five through twenty-seven dollars

Series $\begin{cases} \text{17\%, 22\%, and 37\%} & \text{seventeen, twenty-two, and} \\ & \text{thirty-seven percent} \\ \text{\$25, \$26, and \$27} & \text{twenty-five, twenty-six, and twenty-} \\ & \text{seven dollars} \end{cases}$

Note: When using the number-word form, repeat the word to avoid confusion. See ¶ 714.

TIME OF DAY

724   Formal Style

Times of day in formal writing. In *formal* usage, spell out all times of day.

> half past seven o'clock   half after eight o'clock

Hyphenating times of day. Use a hyphen between the components of a two-word time-of-day expression; use a hyphen between the second and third words in a three-word time-of-day expression.

> eight-thirty   eight thirty-five   twelve forty-nine

O'clock, a.m., p.m. Use *o'clock* with spelled-out numbers (it adds formality) and *a.m.* or *p.m.* with numerals.

> quarter past eight o'clock in the evening   8:15 p.m.

725   General Style

Times not on the half hour. In *general* usage, times of day *not on the half hour* are written in figures. It is proper (except in formal writing) to employ figures anytime the intent is to emphasize accuracy or punctuality.

> 12:17 p.m.   8:32 a.m.

Approximate and even times of day. In *general* usage, approximate and on-the-half-hour times are usually spelled out.

> They will arrive about nine o'clock.
> The show will begin at seven-thirty.

Separating hours and minutes. In writing a time of day in figures, use a colon (without spacing before or after it) to separate hours and minutes. See examples in ¶¶ 725 and 726.

a.m., p.m. Typewritten times of day should be written with *a.m.* or *p.m.* in lowercase letters. Printers usually use small caps.

Typewritten	Printed
12:17 p.m.	12:17 P.M.

On-the-hour times of day. In general usage, it is not necessary to add zeros to on-the-hour times of day.

| 3 p.m. | before 9 and after 10 a.m. |

726   Technical Style

Use numbers to express times of day in technical style. Use *a.m.* or *p.m.*—but not the word *o'clock*.

| 11:47 a.m. | 12:23-12:27 p.m. | 12:27 a.m.-1:03 p.m. |

VOTING RESULTS

727   Voting results are always written in figures.

| 5 to 2 | 43,683 to 15,947 | 7-1 |

NUMBERS AS NUMBERS

728   Numbers referred to as numbers rather than for their numeric *value* are always written in figures.

> Write a 4 in the blank.
> The number you want is 68.

POOR USAGE OF NUMBERS

729   Avoid redundancy, inconsistency, lack of parallelism, etc.

Not:	*But:*
9:00 a.m. in the morning	9:00 a.m., or 9:00 a.m. tomorrow
tomorrow a.m.	tomorrow morning
6 p.m. o'clock	6 p.m., 6:00 p.m., or six o'clock
11:30 p.m. until midnight	11:30 p.m. until 12 midnight
12 noon until midnight	12 noon until 12 midnight
	or
	noon until midnight

Note: Since some instruments do not indicate *noon* or *midnight*, it is sometimes necessary to substitute:

| 12:00 p.m. for noon | 12:00 a.m. for midnight |

WRITING NUMBERS IN FIGURES

730   Commas

Whole numbers of four or more digits may be divided into hundreds, thousands, millions, billions, trillions, etc., by using commas.

three thousand	3,000
forty thousand	40,000
two hundred fifty thousand	250,000
four million two hundred fifty thousand	4,250,000 (Or 4.25 million)
two billion	2,000,000,000 (Or 2 billion)
seventeen trillion	17,000,000,000,000 (Or 17 trillion)

Comma omitted. The comma is frequently omitted in writing four-digit numbers not included in a set containing numbers of five digits or more.

3500   5736   9345   2974

Metric quantities. Use a space instead of a comma in expressing metric quantities. In writing four-digit metric quantities, do not leave such a space unless the number appears in a column with at least one number of five digits or more.

2 456 574		386
475 296		2937
8 594	**But:**	84
7 481 846		8365

731   Stock, Item, Serial, and Policy Numbers

Stock numbers, item numbers, serial numbers, policy numbers, etc., are always written in figures. In general style, they may be preceded by the abbreviation *No.*; in technical style, the symbol # may be used; neither *No.* nor # is *necessary.*

No. 405247093   #402222111   35822220   555 308 33940

WRITING NUMBERS IN WORDS

732   **Hyphenation.** Hyphenate the following.

- All cardinal numbers between 21 and 99 inclusive

  twenty-eight   seventy-six

- All ordinal numbers between 21 and 99 inclusive

  twenty-eighth   seventy-sixth

If a number within this range is part of a larger number (121 or larger), do not use additional hyphens.

> one hundred twenty-eight
> one hundred twenty-eighth
> thirteen hundred eighty-two
> thirteen hundred eighty-second

Unless: Numbers *in the same range* are used again in the same larger number.

> *forty-two* thousand one hundred *fifty-six*

UNIT

8 Business Mathematics

COMPUTING PERCENTAGES

801   Percentage of Increase

To calculate an increase as a percentage, divide the *increase* by the *base*.

This Year's Sales	$318,671	% Increase = $\dfrac{\text{Increase}}{\text{Base}}$
Last Year's Sales	−256,817	
Increase	$ 61,854	% Increase = $\dfrac{61,854}{256,817}$
		% Increase = 24

802   Percentage of Decrease

To calculate a decrease as a percentage, divide the *decrease* by the *base*.

Last Year's Sales	$256,817	% Decrease = $\dfrac{\text{Decrease}}{\text{Base}}$
This Year's Sales	−214,811	
Decrease	$ 42,006	% Decrease = $\dfrac{42,006}{256,817}$
		% Decrease = 16

8

803   Trade Discounts

Trade discounts are discounts allowed by suppliers (wholesalers, distributors, etc.).

List Price	List Price	$9267.50
− Trade Discount	Trade Discount @ 12%	−1112.10
Net Price	Net Price	$8155.40

804   Cash Discount

Business firms selling to other business firms frequently allow a discount if the merchandise is paid for promptly. A *cash discount* of 1 percent or 2 percent may be allowed if the invoice is paid within 10 days. The *terms* are then said to be 2/10, N30: a 2 percent cash discount if paid within 10 days; the full amount is due in 30 days.

Amount of Invoice	$1476.32
− Cash Discount (2%)	− 29.53
Amount Due	$1446.79

Note: If the customer did not pay within 10 days, no cash discount would be allowed, and the amount due would equal the original (gross) amount.

Amount of Invoice	$1476.32
− Discount (none)	− 00.00
Amount Due	$1476.32

805   Chain Discounts

Chain discounts are applied in *sequence*. For example, a supplier may offer a regular trade discount, a special promotional discount, *and* a discount for each additional 100 units sold:

Regular Trade Discount	12%
Special Promotional Discount	3%
100-Unit Discount	2%

Note: Chain discounts cannot be *added*; they must be applied in sequence.

Suppose your firm is purchasing its 201st unit at a list price of $9874.23. The discounts would be 12-3-2-2. (For the simplified method of computing discounts, see ¶ 806 and example below.)

Formula

Base 1 − 12% = Base 2
Base 2 − 3% = Base 3
Base 3 − 2% = Base 4
Base 4 − 2% = Net Price

Regular Method	**Simplified Method**
$9874.23 − 12% = $8689.32	$9874.23 × .88 = $8689.32
$8689.32 − 3% = $8428.64	$8689.32 × .97 = $8428.64
$8428.64 − 2% = $8260.07	$8428.64 × .98 = $8260.07
$8260.07 − 2% = $8094.87	$8260.07 × .98 = $8094.87

If chain discounts could be added, this one would be 19 percent. A 19 percent discount from the list price ($9874.23 − 19%) yields an *erroneous* net price of $7998.13. The *correct* net price is $8094.87.

806   Simplified Method for Computing Discounts

Try the simplified method for computing discounts:

List Price	×	(1.00 − % Discount)	= Net Price
$9874.23	×	(1.00 − .12)	= Net Price
$9874.23	×	(.88)	= Net Price
$9874.23	×	.88	= $8689.32

MARKUP

807   Some suppliers quote wholesale prices rather than offering discounts from list prices. In those cases, the retailer must compute the selling price by adding a *markup* (percentage increase) to the wholesale price.

$$\text{Selling Price} = \text{Wholesale Price} + \left(\begin{matrix} \text{Wholesale} \\ \text{Price} \end{matrix} \times \begin{matrix} \text{Percentage} \\ \text{Markup} \end{matrix} \right)$$

Wholesale Price	$8276.23
Percentage Markup	× .20
$ Markup	$1655.2460
Wholesale Price	+8276.23
Selling Price	$9931.48

Markup—simplified method. Consider the wholesale price as 100 percent of itself and add the markup. Using the data from the markup problem above:

Wholesale Price	100%
Markup	+ 20%
Selling Price	120%

Selling Price = 120% of $8276.23
Selling Price = $9931.48

METRIC TABLES

808   The following tables may be used to convert to and from units of measure used in the metric system.

TABLE 8-1

Metric Units

Basic Metric Units

Quantity	Unit	Symbol
Length	meter	m
Mass	kilogram	kg
Time	second	s
Temperature *	kelvin	K
Electric current	ampere	A
Luminous intensity	candela	cd
Amount of substance	mole	mol
* Common Unit	degree Celsius	°C

Supplementary Metric Units

Quantity	Unit	Symbol
Plane angle	radian	rad
Solid angle	steradian	sr

Derived Metric Units

Quantity	Unit	Symbol	Formula
acceleration	meter per second squared	m/s^2	—
area	square meter	m^2	—
density	kilogram per cubic meter	kg/m^3	—
electric charge	coulomb	C	A•s
electric field strength	volt per meter	V/m	—
electric resistance	ohm	Ω	V/A
energy	joule	J	N•m
force	newton	N	kg•m/s^2
frequency	hertz	Hz	s^{-1}
illumination	lux	lx	lm/m^2
power	watt	W	J/s
pressure	newton per square meter	N/m^2	—
quantity of heat	joule	J	N•m
velocity	meter per second	m/s	—
voltage	volt	V	W/A
volume	cubic meter	m^3	—
work	joule	J	N•m

TABLE 8-2

Metric Prefixes

Value	Power of 10	Prefix		Symbol
1 000 000 000 000	10^{12}	tera	(ter'a)	T
1 000 000 000	10^{9}	giga	(jig'a)	G
1 000 000	10^{6}	mega	(meg'a)	M
1 000	10^{3}	kilo	(kil'o)	k
100	10^{2}	hecto	(hek'to)	h
10	10^{1}	deka	(dek'a)	da
0.1	10^{-1}	deci	(des'i)	d
0.01	10^{-2}	centi	(sen'ti)	c
0.001	10^{-3}	milli	(mil'i)	m
0.000 001	10^{-6}	micro	(mi'kro)	μ
0.000 000 001	10^{-9}	nano	(nan'o)	n
0.000 000 000 001	10^{-12}	pico	(pe'ko)	p

TABLE 8-3

Metric Measurements

area

100	square millimeters	(mm^2)	1	square centimeter	(cm^2)
100	square centimeters	(cm^2)	1	square decimeter	(dm^2)
100	square decimeters	(dm^2)	1	square meter	(m^2)
100	square meters	(m^2)	1	square dekameter	(dam^2)
100	square dekameters	(dam^2)	1	square hectometer	(hm^2)
100	square hectometers	(hm^2)	1	square kilometer	(km^2)

capacity

10	milliliters	(ml)	1	centiliter	(cl)
10	centiliters	(cl)	1	deciliter	(dl)
10	deciliters	(dl)	1	liter	(l)
10	liters	(l)	1	dekaliter	(dal)
10	dekaliters	(dal)	1	hectoliter	(hl)
10	hectoliters	(hl)	1	kiloliter	(kl)
1	cubic decimeter	(dm^3)	1	liter	(l)

length

10	millimeters	(mm)	1	centimeter	(cm)
10	centimeters	(cm)	1	decimeter	(dm)
10	decimeters	(dm)	1	meter	(m)
10	meters	(m)	1	dekameter	(dam)
10	dekameters	(dam)	1	hectometer	(hm)
10	hectometers	(hm)	1	kilometer	(km)

(continued)

TABLE 8-3 (continued)

mass and weight

10 milligrams	(mg)	....	1 centigram	(cg)
10 centigrams	(cg)	....	1 decigram	(dg)
10 decigrams	(dg)	....	1 gram	(g)
10 grams	(g)	....	1 dekagram	(dag)
10 dekagrams	(dag)	....	1 hectogram	(hg)
10 hectograms	(hg)	....	1 kilogram	(kg)
1 cubic decimeter	(dm³)	....	1 liter(l) = 1 kilogram (kg)	

volume

1000 cubic millimeters	(mm³)	....	1 cubic centimeter	(cm³)
1000 cubic centimeters	(cm³)	....	1 cubic decimeter	(dm³)
1000 cubic decimeters	(dm³)	....	1 cubic meter	(m³)

TABLE 8-4

Conversion

Metric English Conversion	English-Metric Conversion
Approximate Values	**Approximate Values**
1 mm .... 0.04 inch	1 inch .... 25.4 mm
1 cm .... 0.4 inch	1 inch .... 2.54 cm
1 m .... 39.37 inches	1 foot .... 0.305 m
1 km .... 0.6 mile	1 yard .... 0.91 m
	1 mile .... 1.61 km
1 cm² .... 0.16 square inch	
1 m² .... 10.8 square feet	1 square inch ..... 6.5 cm²
1 m² .... 1.2 square yards	1 square foot ...... 0.09 m²
1 hectare .... 2.5 acres	1 square yard 0.8m²
	1 acre .... 0.4 hectare
1 cm³ .... 0.06 cubic inch	
1 m³ .... 35.3 cubic feet	1 cubic inch ...... 16.4 cm³
1 m³ .... 1.3 cubic yards	1 cubic foot .... 0.03 m³
	1 cubic yard ...... 0.8 m³
1 ml .... 0.034 ounce	
1 cl .... 0.34 ounce	1 pint .... 0.47 l
1 l .... 2.1 pints	1 quart .... 0.95 l
1 l .... 1.06 quarts	1 gallon .... 3.79 l
1 l .... 0.26 gallon	1 ounce .... 28.35 g
1 g .... 0.035 ounce	1 pound .... 0.45 kg
1 kg .... 2.2 pounds	1 U.S. ton .... 0.9 metric ton
1 metric t .... 1.1 U.S. ton	

TABLE 8-5

Temperature

Celsius		Fahrenheit
0°C	freezing point of water	32°F
10°C	a spring day	50°F
20°C	recommended indoor temperature	68°F
30°C	a summer day	86°F
37°C	body temperature	98.6°F
100°C	boiling point of water	212°F

Converting from Fahrenheit to Celsius

$$C = \frac{5}{9} (F - 32)$$

Converting from Celsius to Fahrenheit

$$F = \frac{9}{5} C + 32$$

Typing Basics

901   This unit reviews some areas that you probably will recall from beginning typing. An occasional refresher is a good idea when you haven't used a particular skill for awhile. But while the information on horizontal and vertical centering and tabulation may be a review, the section on making corrections contains the latest in correction techniques.

HORIZONTAL CENTERING

902   *Horizontal centering*—centering a line from side to side—is the term used for centering a line in relation to the side edges of the paper. You probably use horizontal centering most often to center a line in typed material.

9

903   **Steps for Horizontal Centering**

1. Find the horizontal center of the paper.

Scale reading for left edge of paper
+ Scale reading for right edge of paper
───────────────────────────
Total ÷ 2 = Center Point

Examples

Elite	*Pica*
0	0
+ 102	+ 85
102/2 = 51	85/2 = 42
	(Ignore leftover fraction)

2. Move margin stops to far left and right of scale.

3. If you have several lines to center, clear all tab stops and set tab stop at center. Only one line to center? Simply space to center.

4. From the center, backspace once for every two letters, spaces, figures, or punctuation marks in the line to be centered.

5. Do not backspace for one leftover stroke at the end of the line.

6. Begin to type the line where your backspacing ends.

Note: For centering on odd-size paper and cards, the same steps are used.

904   Spread Headings

A *spread heading* looks like this:

$$W \ O \ R \ D \qquad S \ T \ U \ D \ I \ E \ S$$

To type a spread heading:

1. Backspace from center once for *each* letter, space, figure, or punctuation mark, except the last letter or character in the heading. Begin to type where the backspacing ends.

2. When typing the spread heading, space once after each letter or character and three times between words.

VERTICAL CENTERING

905   *Vertical centering*—also called *top to bottom centering*—is the term used for centering one or several lines in relation to the top and bottom edges of the paper. You probably use this skill most often in typing tabulated material.

9

906   Steps for Vertical Centering

Backspace from center method.

1. Find the vertical center of the paper.

   Full sheet typing paper = 11 inches long × 6 lines per inch = 66 total lines. Space from the top edge of the paper down 11 TS (triple spaces) + 1 SS (single space) (line 34).

Half sheet typing paper = 5½ inches × 6 lines per inch = 33 total lines. Space from the top edge of the paper down 6 TS − 1 SS (line 17).

2. From the vertical center of the paper, roll the platen (cylinder) back one time for every two lines, two blank line spaces, or line and blank line combination. Ignore odd or leftover lines.

Remember:	Single-spacing	= no blank lines	Triple-spacing	= two - - - - - - - - blank - - - - - - - - lines
	Double-spacing	= one - - - - blank - - - - line		

Mathematical method.

1. Count the total lines + the blank lines needed to type the entire problem.

2. Subtract the total lines to be used from 66 (full sheet) or 33 (half sheet).

3. Divide by two to get the top and bottom margins, disregarding fractions. This tells you the total number of *blank* lines to be left at the top of the page. Begin typing *on the next line*.

$$\frac{\text{Total Lines} - \text{Lines to be Used}}{2} = \text{top margin; begin typing on next line}$$

Note: For vertical centering on odd-size paper or cards, determine the total lines available by multiplying total inches long by six. Then follow the steps indicated above.

Reading position. When centering vertically on whole sheets of paper or half sheets with the long edge of the paper at the left, it is preferable sometimes to set the paper for *reading position*. Material that is exactly centered vertically tends to look too low because of optical illusion. *Reading position* compensates for this illusion by positioning the material two lines higher than the exact vertical center. To set for reading position, set the material for exact vertical centering and subtract two lines (roll the platen back two additional single spaces).

TABULATION

907   *Tabulation* is the term used to represent the typing of columns of information. Illustration 9-1 shows a simple table with a main heading, secondary heading, and column headings. Tabulation is a way to present complex information in columns for easy reading and comparisons.

ILLUSTRATION 9-1

Sample Typed Table

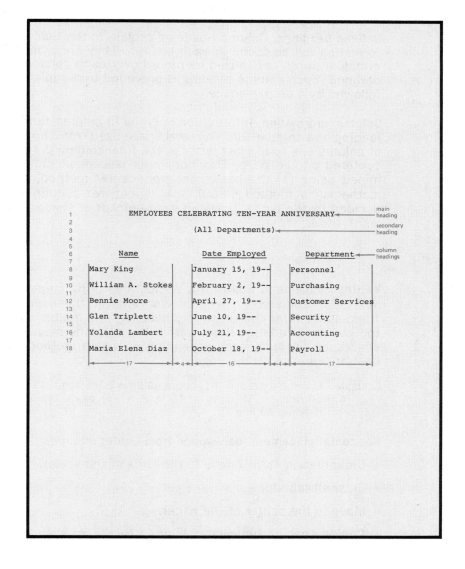

908   Elements of a Table

Headings. Two types of headings are often used in tabulations: a main heading typed all in caps and a secondary heading with only the first letter of each principal word capitalized. (See Unit 4, Capitalization, for more information.) If a main heading is used alone, a triple space (leaving two blank lines) follows before column headings or column information. When both a main and secondary heading are used (as in Illustration 9-1), a double space follows the main heading, with a triple space following the secondary heading. Main headings describe information to be found in a table; secondary headings further clarify the main heading. Both main and secondary headings may be centered horizontally.

Column headings. Column headings explain to the reader what information will be found in each column. They are typed with the principal words capitalized, centered over each column, and underlined. Each column heading is preceded by a triple space and followed by a double space.

Column information. Information is typed in column form for easy reading and comparison. The total space used from the first letter of column one to the last letter of the final column is horizontally centered on the page. This horizontal placement can be determined using (1) the backspace-from-center method, or (2) the mathematical method (¶ 909). Spacing between columns is usually decided by the typist, using an even number of spaces (four, six, eight, etc.).

909   Typing a Table

Vertical placement. Follow the vertical centering steps explained in ¶ 906. Remember to double-space after the main heading, triple-space after the secondary heading, and double-space after the column headings. Items within the columns may be double-spaced or single-spaced, depending on which method gives the best appearance on the page.

Example: Using Illustration 9-1, count all lines to be used (18 total lines). 66 lines − 18 lines = 48 ÷ 2 = 24; begin typing the main heading on line 25.

Horizontal placement (backspace-from-center method).

• Clear margin stops (move to the ends of the scale).

• Clear all tab stops.

• Move to the center of the paper.

• Decide spacing between columns (usually an even number of

spaces: four, six, etc.).

- Find the longest line in each column.

- Find and set the left margin stop. Backspace from the center of the paper one space for each two letters, figures, symbols, and spaces in the longest line of each column, and for each two spaces between columns. Set the left margin at this point.

- Find and set the tab stops. From the left margin, space forward one space for each letter, figure, symbol, and space in the longest line in the first column, and for the space between columns one and two. Set a tab stop at this point for column two. Follow similar steps when additional columns are to be typed.

Example:

William A. Stokes	February 2, 19--	Customer Services
17	4	16	4	17

William A. Stokes 1 2 3 4 February 2, 19-- 1 2 3 4 Customer Services

Horizontal placement (mathematical method).

- Clear margin stops (move to the ends of the scale).

- Clear all tab stops.

- Move to the center of the paper.

- Decide spacing between columns (usually an even number of spaces: four, six, etc.).

- Find the longest line in each column.

- Find and set the left margin stop. Add the longest line in each column to the spaces between the columns. Divide by two. Subtract from the center. Set the left margin at this point.

- Find and set the tab stops. From the left margin, space forward one space for each letter, figure, symbol, and space in the longest line in the first column, and for the space between columns one and two. Set a tab stop at this point for column two. Follow similar steps when additional columns are to be typed.

Example:

William A. Stokes	February 2, 19--	Customer Services
17	+	4	+	16	+	4	+	17 = 58

$$58 \div 2 = 29$$

	Elite	*Pica*
	51	42
	−29	−29
	22	13 = Left Margin

Centering column headings. Column headings are centered above each column. This process is simple if you recall the procedures for horizontal centering: move to the center; backspace once for every two letters, figures, symbols, and spaces. To center the column heading, simply move to the center of the column and backspace.

- To find the center of the column:
  From the point where the column begins, space forward once for each two letters, figures, symbols, or spaces *in the longest line in the column*.

- To center the column heading:
  From the center of the column, backspace once for each two letters, figures, symbols, and spaces *in the column heading*. Type the heading. Underline the column heading. Double-space and begin the column information.

910   Tabulation in Business Letters and Manuscripts

Detailed material in letters and reports may be easier to understand if it is tabulated. When this occurs, the tabulated material is typed after double-spacing below the preceding paragraph. Double-spacing is also used after the tabulated material, before continuing the remainder of the letter or manuscript. See Illustration 9-2 for an example of a memo containing tabulated material.

911   Ruled Columns

Sometimes information provided in tabulated columns becomes very complicated. When this occurs, it often helps to arrange column information with ruled lines so the reader can read the column more easily. An example of a complex ruled column is presented in Illustration 9-3. To type a ruled column, follow vertical and horizontal centering discussed previously. After the tabulation is completely typed, insert the lines.

To draw horizontal lines on the typewriter, place the pencil or pen point through the hole or notch in the card holder (or on the type bar guide above the ribbon); depress the carriage-release lever (clear all tabs and use tab key for Selectrics) to draw the line across the page. For double-line rulings, type (or draw) the first line; then use the variable line spacer to move the paper forward slightly. Type (or draw) the second horizontal line.

To draw vertical lines on the typewriter, operate the automatic line finder. Place the pencil or pen point through the cardholder. Roll the paper up until you have a line of the desired length. Remove the pen or pencil and remember to reset the line finder.

ILLUSTRATION 9-2 Sample Memorandum with Table

M E M O R A N D U M

TO: Dr. Horace Traylor
    Employee Relations

FROM: Dr. Marie Hydress
      Personnel

DATE: July 12, 19--

SUBJECT: Ten-Year Pins

Thank you for offering to order the ten-year pins for employees celebrating their tenth anniversary with Gonzalez & Co. The same style pins as were used last year will be fine with the exception of the change in color to blue, as we discussed.

Following is a listing of employees' names for engraving on each pin:

Name	Date Employed	Department
Mary King	January 15, 19--	Personnel
William A. Stokes	February 2, 19--	Purchasing
Bennie Moore	April 27, 19--	Customer Services
Glen Triplett	June 10, 19--	Security
Yolanda Lambert	July 21, 19--	Accounting
Maria Elena Diaz	October 18, 19--	Payroll

Please call me when the pins arrive, and I will arrange to have them picked up and gift wrapped for each employee. Thanks again for your help.

mos

ILLUSTRATION 9-3 Sample Ruled Table

SCHOOL — Name, Address, and Contact	Faculty — View Sample	Faculty — Ext/Unsatisfied	Faculty — Unsatisfied	Faculty — Satisfied	Faculty — Ext/Enthusiastic	Faculty — Enthusiastic	Students — Ext/Unsatisfied	Students — Unsatisfied	Students — Satisfied	Students — Ext/Enthusiastic	Students — Enthusiastic	Use — Research	Use — Article	From — Combination	From — Open Lab	From — Trad. Classroom	How — Detailed Script	How — Abbrev. Script	How — Detailed L. Plan	How — Brief L. Plan	How — Another School	How — Locally Prepared	How — Commer. Prepared	Type — Slides	Type — Film	Type — Closed Circuit TV	Type — Video Tapes
Loop College, 64 E. Lake, Chicago IL 60601-7529, Mr. Guy Richards				X		X			X	X	X		X	X								X	X	X		X	X
Heald Colleges, 1255 Post Street, San Francisco CA 94101-2137, Dr. Jim Deitz	X			X		X			X	X			X	X								X	X	X			X
University of Tennessee, Business Education Department, Knoxville TN 37916-4419, Dr. E. Ray Smith & Dr. Dan Reese	X			X		X		X	X	X			X	X								X	X	X		X	X

PROOFREADING

912   Some of the time spent making corrections can be eliminated by careful proofreading of typed material *while it is still in the type-writer.*
Hints for accurate proofreading:

- Take your time. Proofread slowly.

- It helps to read aloud.

- Proofread each page while it is still in the typewriter, line by line, using your carriage return.

- When proofreading for spelling, read the material backwards.

- Be on the lookout for these common errors:

    Errors in format
    Errors in content
    Errors in use of materials

Proofreader's marks. Proofreader's marks are used not only by those who read proof for publishers and printers, but also by almost all people who have occasion to indicate corrections in type-written or printed material.
Proofreaders' marks are sometimes applied directly to the location of the change.

Before Change   **After Change**

when i̲ move   when I move

I when move   when I move

Proofreaders' marks may appear in the margins instead of at the location of the change. When these marginal marks are used, supplementary marks *in the text* indicate the location of the change.

Change	Marginal Mark	Supplementary Mark in Text	After Change
Align	‖	words on a list	words on a list
Capitalize	(Cap)	new york	New York
Close up space	⌒	win ter	winter

Change	Marginal Mark	Supplementary Mark in Text	After Change
Delete	ꝰ	leave ~~out~~ the	leave the
Delete and close up space	ꝰ	peoople	people
Insert	out	leave the	leave out the
Insert apostrophe	ⱴ	Maries dress	Marie's dress
Insert asterisk	ⱴ	the end, but	the end,* but
Insert brackets	[/]	run fast now	run /fast/ now
Insert colon	⌃	follow these steps	follow these steps:
Insert comma	⌄	ham, eggs and toast	ham, eggs, and toast
Insert diagonal	⊘	and or the former	and/or the former
Insert hyphen	⹀	do it yourself project	do-it-yourself project
Insert parenthesis	(/)	run fast now	run (fast) now
Insert period	⊙	the end	the end.
Insert quotation marks	ⱴ/ⱴ	the end.	the "end."
Insert semicolon	⌃	Row, row, row.	Row; row; row.
Insert space	#	thespace	the space
Let stand	stet	~~best~~ well-wisher	best well-wisher
Lowercase	lc	the Summer season	the summer season
Move down	⌴	dow^n	down
Move left	[	move [left	move left
Move right	]	move right]	move right
Move up	⌐	u_p	up
Spell out	sp	wouldn't run	would not run
Start a paragraph	¶	¶The first line and the second	The first line and the second
Straighten the line	═	straighten the line	straighten the line
Transpose	tr	first to strike	to strike first

CORRECTIONS

913   *Even the best typists make errors.* Therefore, the typist, together with the employer, must decide what type of correcting technique to use—automatic typewriters, self-correcting typewriters, typewriters with lift-off correcting ribbon, erasing, correction paper, correction fluid, or correction tape. Listed below are the important features of each correcting technique.

914   **Automatic Typewriters**

Automatic typewriters are those which use magnetic cards, tapes, disks, memory, and/or computer storage to record typed material. Typing errors are corrected by backspacing and typing the correct characters over the errors. Once the correction has been made, the original error is no longer recorded.

915   **Self-Correcting Typewriters**

Self-correcting typewriters are designed with a correction key and correction ribbon. Errors are lifted off the page or covered with a chalk-like substance. Self-correcting typewriters with a lift-off correction ribbon are by far the fastest, easiest, and neatest method of error correction on originals. A lift-off typewriter ribbon, including lift-off correction tabs, may be available for your make and model of typewriter. Check with your local office supply store for information on your particular machine.

916   **Erasing**

Erasing is one of the oldest forms of correction. Pink or grey rubber typing erasers are available. The grey eraser contains more abrasive material than the pink eraser and should be used with high-quality bond paper. Use the pink eraser with thinner quality paper to avoid erasing a hole in the paper.

Trick of the trade. A quick cleaning method for erasers is to run your dirty eraser along the rough edge of an emery board or sandpaper. Fiberglass erasers are useful on thick card stock, such as 5" × 3" cards. Electric and battery operated erasers can also be used for card stock but are designed primarily for drafting work.

Note: Chalk or white pencil can be used to put the "white" back in paper after an erasure has noticeably damaged the surrounding area.

917   **Correction Paper**

Correction paper is essentially paper with a chalk-like, white substance on one side. Correction paper comes in a variety of forms, including rolls, small tabs, and tear-off sheets. In addition, some manufacturers also provide colored correction paper for corrections on colored stationery and carbon correction paper for carbon copy errors. Like an eraser, correction paper is both inexpensive and portable. Correction paper is not considered a permanent correction method. Some brands tend to flake off.

Trick of the trade. If correction paper does not completely cover an error, use a square of transparency film over the correction paper for a denser, thicker covering.

918   Correction Fluid

Correction fluid usually comes in bottles with a brush in the cap. Basically, this opaque fluid is used to cover the error. Steps should be taken to keep the fluid thin with either a chemical thinner (for chemical-base fluid) or water (for water-base fluid). Skill should be acquired in "dotting on" correction fluid to avoid the obvious "painted" correction.

Note: Correction fluid is available in colors for colored stationery, in a pen-like holder, and as a special fluid for corrections on photocopies.

919   Correction Tape

Correction tape is white pressure-sensitive adhesive paper, usually available in rolls, and can be used for covering a word, a line, or an entire paragraph. Correction tape is portable and inexpensive. This correction method, however, is *very* obvious and should not be used for copies that are to be distributed. It is excellent for copies prepared for reproduction.

Trick of the trade. To avoid "lines" on photocopies from correction tape, use correction fluid to paint out the edges of the tape.

920   Erasable Paper

Erasable paper has been treated with chemicals to make errors easy to erase. This type of paper is seldom used in business, since it is more expensive than regular bond paper and handling a letter might smear the freshly typed page. Typists do consider the use of this special paper for reports and other lengthy typing jobs.

921   Carbon Copy Corrections

Unfortunately, the new developments in the self-correcting typewriter and lift-off ribbon do not help with carbon copy errors.

Carbon copy errors should be corrected with erasing, correction paper, and/or correction fluid.

When *erasing* carbon copy errors, protect all following carbon copies by using a stiff card or erasing shield (a long piece of metal curved like the platen) in *front* of the following carbon, immediately *behind* the error being erased.

Correction paper must be used in front of *each* carbon copy error and removed before retyping the correction.

If *correction fluid* is used, "dot out" each carbon copy error. Let the fluid dry thoroughly before moving on to other corrections to avoid having the fluid adhere to the carbon paper rather than to the copy.

922   NCR and Other Carbonless Paper

NCR (No Carbon Required) and other carbonless paper is treated with chemicals causing typed letters to appear on the copy either from the back of the preceding sheet or from within the sheet itself. There is no way to correct errors made on this type of paper except with a pen, pencil, or strikeover.

923   Material Removed from the Typewriter

Errors discovered after pages have been removed from the typewriter take longer to correct. Use the typewriter alignment scale to realign the page horizontally and vertically.

Trick of the trade. Letters such as *i* and *l* will closely line up with the vertical lines on the alignment scale. To check the alignment before typing the correction, type with the window of a window envelope in front of the page first.

Each carbon copy must be reinserted and corrected separately; it is not possible to reinsert and align the original carbon pack.

Trick of the trade. Make reinserted carbon corrections undetectable by placing a stapled square of bond paper and carbon paper in front of the correction before retyping.

924   Corrections on Bound Copies

Top-bound copies can be corrected by realignment in the typewriter. Insert a separate sheet of paper, rolling forward until one inch is showing in front of the platen; place the bound copy page with the error behind the sheet, in front of the platen; roll the sheet backward out of the machine; the bound page will roll into the typewriter. Realign and correct the error.

Trick of the trade. *Side-bound copies* can be corrected using rub-on letters available in pica and elite from office supply stores.

925   Squeezing and Spreading Letters

When the correction of a word contains one *more* letter than the original word, you must *squeeze* letters together to fit the original space. By beginning the first letter of a word and all following letters a half-space to the left, it is possible to fit an extra letter into the word.

When the correction of a word contains one *less* letter than the original word, you must *spread* letters and spaces apart to make your correction undetectable. By beginning the first letter of a word and all following letters a half-space to the right (moving the typewriter carriage by using the carriage release key), the extra space left from the omitted letter will be taken up at the beginning and end of the word.

Note: To squeeze and spread on a typewriter with an element, simply push the element carrier to the left a half-space, using the red typing position indicator as a guide.

Perfect corrections require *perfect* correction methods. Practice with all of the methods indicated above will help you determine what combination works best for you.

Table 9-1 summarizes for your visual inspection all of the foregoing statements concerning correction techniques. Refer to it as often as necessary!

TYPING FORMS

926   Information on forms—such as applications, invoices, bills of lading, etc.—should be typed on the lines of the form so that only a slight space separates the letters from the underline (about the width of a hair). To give the forms you complete a professional look, align the beginnings of typed lines where possible. Fill in all requested information, inserting N/A (not applicable) or a dash for lines which do not apply.

TYPING INDEX CARDS AND LABELS

927   Index cards and labels tend to slip as you type them. Solve this problem by making a small pleat, 1/4 inch wide, in a sheet of typing paper. Use cellophane tape to tape the ends of the pleat. Insert index cards or labels in the pleat and roll the sheet into the typewriter. Slippage will be eliminated.

TABLE 9-1

Making the Correction Choice

CORRECTION CHOICES / CONSIDERATIONS	Automatic Typewriter	Self-Correcting Typewriter	Lift-Off Ribbon with Tabs	Erasing	Correction Paper	Correction Fluid	Correction Tape
Time	Very fast	Very fast	Fast	Slowest if done correctly	Fast	Slow when "dotting"	Fast
Correction Quality—Originals	Excellent	Excellent	Excellent	Excellent if done correctly	Good when retyping; poor to cover space	Good when retyping; poor to cover space	Poor; obvious correction
Carbon Copies	Will not correct	Will not correct	Will not correct	Excellent; use soft eraser	Special paper for carbons	Good; allow time to dry	Poor; obvious correction
Photocopies	Will not correct	Will not correct	Will not correct	Eraser sometimes smears	Will not correct	Use water-based fluid	Poor; obvious correction
Problems	Expense of equipment	Expense of correcting feature and supplies	Expense of lift-off ribbon and tabs	Time-consuming	Chalk-like covering sometimes flakes	"dotting-on" for good correction takes time	Poor; obvious correction
Special Advantages	Storage method remembers only corrections	Fast, neat method	Fast, neat method	Portable, inexpensive	Portable, inexpensive	Portable, inexpensive	Excellent for changing letters, words, and lines on material to be photocopied

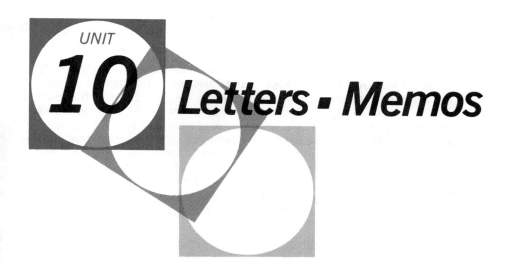

UNIT 10
Letters • Memos

This unit provides information on two essentials in the business office: the business letter and the interoffice memorandum. Letters are the most common form of written communication in the business office. Rising costs of stationery, envelopes, postage, the secretary's and originator's time, and office overhead have all contributed to the increased cost of business letter preparation. It is the secretary's responsibility to help maintain accuracy, neatness, and efficiency in the preparation of letters and interoffice memorandums.

PARTS OF A BUSINESS LETTER

1001   All business letters have certain essential elements. In addition, other elements may or may not be included, depending on letter requirements.

Required

- Letterhead or Return Address
- Date
- Inside Address
- Salutation (not required for AMS Simplified)
- Body
- Complimentary Close (not required for AMS Simplified)
- Originator's Identification
- Reference Initials

Optional

- Mailing/Special Notations
- Attention Line
- Subject Line
- Typed Company Name
- Title of Originator
- Enclosure Notation
- Carbon Copy Notation
- Postscript

10

1002   Appearance

Before discussing the parts of a business letter, it is necessary to point out one of the most essential characteristics of written communications in the office—*appearance*. Frequently the only contact a customer will have with your office is through business letters. If the letter is not accurately and neatly typed, the appearance will distract the reader from the message. It is important that you look your best when meeting a new customer for the first time. Apply the same principle to the business letter. Neat corrections, attractive placement, and correct grammar, punctuation, and spelling techniques help your business letter make a good first impression. (Letter placement is discussed in detail in ¶ 1004.)

1003   Letterhead/Return Address

In most business offices, out-of-company letters are typed on a high-quality bond letterhead paper. Letterheads help create the reader's impression of the organization, and vary in quality as well as complexity. Approximately 1½-2 inches is taken up by the letterhead design. Illustrations 10-1 and 10-2 are two examples of both simple and complex designs. Note that both contain the company name, street address, city, two-letter state abbreviation and ZIP Code. Telephone numbers are considered desirable.

ILLUSTRATION 10-1

Letterhead with Date Beginning at Center

10

ILLUSTRATION 10-2

Letterhead with Date Ending at Right Margin

When typing a *personal* business letter, use your home address as a letterhead; type as follows:

> 1610 Midvale Avenue
> Los Angeles, CA 90024–4738
> July 12, 19––

Examples of personal letters are shown in Unit 1, Illustrations 1-1 and 1-2. The return address and date in a personal letter can be typed beginning at center, ending at the right margin, or beginning at the left margin. The placement of the return address and date should agree with the letter style chosen. Letter styles are discussed in ¶ 1019. A sample letterhead, plus an illustration of all of the letter parts to be discussed is included in Illustration 10-3.

1004   **Margins**

Letter placement should become an intuitive process. Until the eye has been trained to make accurate judgments, however, a placement table can be quite helpful. Placement of letters is based largely upon their length; variation in letterheads, content, structure, and style must be taken into consideration when a setup is being planned. Each letter should be treated individually.

In determining letter placement, the first step is to recognize and classify the length of the letter. You will need some practice in making these estimates from longhand materials, from shorthand notes, or from a dictating machine. Most placement tables classify letters as short, average, long, and two-page.

When a letter contains a table, quoted material, subject and attention lines, or other unusual features, the total letter length will be increased. Remember to consider these features in determining letter length.

There are two typewriter type sizes: pica and elite.

1. On a typewriter with pica (large) type, there are 10 spaces to a horizontal inch.

2. On a typewriter with elite (small) type, there are 12 spaces to a horizontal inch.

3. Line length may be stated in inches or in spaces per line— or described by stating the width of the margins.

TABLE 10-1

Margin Guide

Letter Length	Width of Margins	Spaces in Margins		Line Length	Spaces in Line	
		Pica	Elite		Pica	Elite
Long	1″	10	12	6½″	65	78
Medium	1½″	15	18	5½″	55	66
Short	2″	20	24	4½″	45	54

The bottom margin will vary depending on the number of words in the letter. Always leave a bottom margin of at least six lines (one inch).

ILLUSTRATION 10-3

Modified Block Style Letter

```
                    The Example Company
Letterhead
                 4900 Drake Road • Bartlett, TN 38134-2245


Dateline                     Line 12            →July 12, 19--
                                 DS
Mailing  →CONFIDENTIAL
Special
Notations             DS
          Take Charge Industries
Attention→Attention Mrs. Ellen Nye
Line
          255 Blue Hill Avenue
Inside ——→Boston, MA 02187-2558
Address               DS
Salutation→Ladies and Gentlemen:
                      DS
Subject——→MODIFIED BLOCK STYLE LETTER
Line
              DS
          This letter is an example of the modified block style with block
          paragraphs.  It is one of the most popular business letter styles
Body      in use today.  You will note that the dateline and closing lines
of   ———→are indented and blocked at the center of the page.  Mixed punc-
Letter    tuation is frequently used with this letter style:  a colon after
          the salutation and a comma after the complimentary close.

          When the modified block style is used, letter production efficiency
          dictates that the dateline, the complimentary close, the company
          name, and the typed name and title of the originator be started at
          the center of the page.
              DS
          This letter is also unusual in that it is loaded with special
          features.  Normally, all illustrations here do not appear within
          one business letter.  However, they are included here to show
          their order within the business letter.
                   DS
Complimentary Close ———————→Sincerely,
                            DS
Company Name ———————————→THE EXAMPLE COMPANY
                            Return 4 Times


Name of Originator ——————→Mario Hernandez-Fumero
Title of Originator ———————→President
                            DS
Reference
Initials ——→mos
              DS
Enclosure →Enclosures
Notation
              DS
Carbon   →cc Ms. Mary King
Copy
Notation      DS
          Please request additional information on business letter stationery
Postscript→from our home office.
```

1005   Date

Floating dateline. Two methods of determining the placement of the date are widely used. The one used most often is the *floating* *dateline*—a dateline that "floats" or varies in vertical position according to the letter length. The length of the letter determines (1) how far down from the top edge of the paper to type the date and (2) the width of the side margins (in inches). The first line of the inside address is always typed on the fourth line below the date. See Table 10-2.

TABLE 10-2

Letter Placement Guide (Floating Dateline)

Letter Classification	5-Stroke Words in Letter Body	Side Margins	Margin Settings		Dateline Position (From Top Edge of Paper)
			Elite	Pica	
Short	Up to 125	2"	24-78*	20-65*	19
Average	126-225	1½"	18-84*	15-70*	16
Long	226-325	1"	12-90*	10-75*	13
Two-page	More than 325	1"	12-90*	10-75*	13
Standard 6" line for all letters **	As above for all letters	1¼"	15-87*	12-72*	As above for all letters

*Plus 3 to 7 spaces for the bell cue—*usually, add 5.*
**Use only when so directed. Some business firms use a standard 6" line for all letters.
Source: T. James Crawford, Lawrence W. Erickson, Lee R. Beaumont, Jerry W. Robinson, and Arnola C. Ownby, *Century 21 Typewriting*, 3d ed. (Cincinnati: South-Western Publishing Co., 1982), p. 143.

Fixed dateline. The second method is the *fixed dateline*—a dateline that is always typed on the second line below the last line of the printed letterhead. In this case, the length of the letter determines (1) the number of blank lines to be left between the date and the inside address and (2) the length of the typed lines within the body of the letter. See Table 10-3.

TABLE 10-3

Letter Placement Guide (Fixed Dateline)

Letter Classification	5-Stroke Words in Letter Body	Variable Margins			Standard 60-Space Line
		Length of Line		Blank Lines Between Date-line and Address **	Blank Lines (Average) Between Dateline and Address **
		Pica Spaces	Elite Spaces		
Short	Up to 125	50*	50*	7-11	8
Average	126-225	60*	60*	3-7	5
Long	226-325	60	70	3-5	3
Two-page	More than 325	60	70	3-5	3

* When it is necessary to change the length of line from a 50-space line to a 60-space line, just move each margin stop out 5 spaces; time can be saved in a similar way when it is necessary to shorten the length of the line.
** Letters at the extremes of the classifications, in terms of the number of words in the body of the letter, may at times require some modification of the suggested spacing between the dateline and the address.

ILLUSTRATION 10-4

Short, Average, and Long Letters with Floating Dateline

 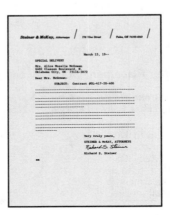 

1006   Letter Adjustments

To *lengthen a short letter* (under 70 words), use any combination of the following:

- Lower the dateline.
- Leave extra lines between the date and inside address.
- Leave four to six lines for the signature.
- Put the originator's name and title on separate lines.
- Leave extra lines before and between reference initials, carbon copy and enclosure notations, and postscripts.

To *shorten a long letter* (over 225 words), use any combination of the following:

- Raise the date.
- Leave fewer lines between the date and inside address.
- Leave only two blank lines for a signature.
- Raise reference initials one or two lines.

1007   Mailing Notations/Other Special Notations

Special mailing instructions, such as AIRMAIL (with foreign mail only), REGISTERED, CERTIFIED, etc., are typed at the left margin of the letter in capitals, a double space below the dateline. Other special notations, such as PERSONAL or CONFIDENTIAL, are typed in the same location in capitals. (See Illustration 10-3.)

1008   Inside Address and Salutation

The inside address and salutation are discussed together because one is dependent upon the other. The *inside address* pro-

ILLUSTRATION 10-5

Short, Average, and Long Letters with Fixed Dateline

vides all necessary information for mail delivery of the letter: name, title, company name, street number and name, city, two-letter state abbreviation, and ZIP Code. (For two-letter state abbreviations, see Unit 5, Table 5-1.) Examples of several inside addresses and appropriate salutations are provided below. Note that the city, state abbreviation, and ZIP Code are typed on one line with two spaces, but no comma, between the state abbreviation and the ZIP Code.

To an Individual (examples of mixed punctuation; colon after salutation)

Ms. Janice Turbett
1150 N. Franklin Avenue
Dearborn, MI 48128-9010

Dear Ms. Turbett:

Mr. Albert W. Clemons, Jr.
Meads Creek Road, R. D. 4
Painted Post, NY 14870-7852

Dear Albert:

To an Individual at a Business Address (examples of open punctuation; no punctuation after salutation)

Dr. Horace E. Traylor
Instructional Resources
Los Angeles Pierce College
6201 Winnetka Avenue
Woodland, CA 91364-1463

Dear Dr. Traylor

Dean of Instruction
Los Angeles Pierce College
6201 Winnetka Avenue
Woodland, CA 91364-1463

Dear Sir or Madam

Two-Line Address

Mrs. Leota Schramm
Rogers City, MI 49779-1627

Dear Aunt Leota

With Apartment Number

Miss Ileana Gonzalez
7131 Wood Drive, Apt. 151
Austin, TX 78731-4325

Dear Ileana

Two People, Different Addresses

Mr. Ray Larson   and   Mrs. Karen McMeekin
P.O. Box 2143   4408 Glen Rose Street
Riverview Road   Fairfax, VA 22032–3216
Riverton, WY 82501–8199

Dear Ray and Karen:

Title Position

Miss Lillie Pinkney, President   Mr. John Ryland
Pinkney's Contracting   Vice–President
13254 Kit Lane   Pinkney's Contracting
Fort Worth, TX 75240–2617   13254 Kit Lane
                                     Fort Worth, TX 75240–2617
Ms. Amy Fisher
Vice–President and   Dear Mr. Ryland
    General Manager
Pinkney's Contracting
13254 Kit Lane
Fort Worth, TX 75240–2617

- Change the position of titles to balance the inside address.

- Additional information on titles, names, and salutations can be found in Special Salutations, ¶ 1022, and Capitalization, ¶ 419.

- When house or building numbers consist of the digit 1 (one), spell out "One"; use figures for other single digits.

> One Metro Boulevard
> 3 Willowtree Lane

Room, Suite, Building in Address

Ms. Juanita Cordova   Columbus Employees Federal
Attorney at Law   Credit Union
429 Broad Street, Suite 41   Penobscot Building, Room 118
Richmond, VA 23219–2183   1800 King Avenue
                                     Columbus, OH 48216–3615
Dear Ms. Cordova:
                                     Ladies and Gentlemen:

- When addressing any organization employing both male and female employees, the correct salutation is *Ladies and Gentlemen*.

- Long company names can be split and put on two lines, indenting the second line two or three spaces.

Two People, Same Address

- Eliminate official titles, unless they are short and can fit on the same line with the name. Omit department, unless both are from the same department. (On individual envelopes, however, type full addresses.)

```
Ms. Gail Cook
Ms. Sarah McDaniel
Editorial Department
South-Western Publishing Co.
5101 Madison Road
Cincinnati, OH  45227-9601

    Dear Ms. Cook and Ms. McDaniel:
```

Husband and Wife   **Foreign Country**

```
Dr. and Mrs. Walter Brundage      Mr. Shawn Carney
Plaza Medical Center              Herts Office Interiors, Ltd.
2050 Massachusetts Avenue         27 Monks Close
Washington, D.C.  20503-5164      Leeds, York  ALY-372
                                  ENGLAND


Dear Dr. and Mrs. Brundage        Dear Mr. Carney:
```

- Type the name of a foreign country on the last line of the inside address in capitals.

In Care Of

```
Dr. Alberta Goodman
In care of Dr. John Rouche        or    c/o Dr. John Rouche
University of Texas at Austin
Austin, TX  78731-3341

Dear Dr. Goodman:
```

1009   Attention Line

Frequently, when a letter is addressed to a company, an *attention line* is used to route the letter to a particular person. The attention line indicates that the letter concerns company business and that the writer prefers that the letter be handled by the individual named in the attention line. The attention line is typed at the left margin as the second item in the inside address. The word *attention* should not be abbreviated. Either of the forms indicated below is acceptable. Please note, however, that the salutation always agrees with the inside address, not the attention line.

```
Carolina Labs                     Alberto-Culver Company
Attention John Sikes              ATTENTION DR. MONICA BELL
1005 Ala Lililoi Street           2525 W. Armitage Avenue
Honolulu, HI  96818-7116          Melrose Park, IL  60164-2648

Ladies and Gentlemen:             Ladies and Gentlemen
```

For an example of the attention line in a business letter, see Illustration 10-3.

1010   Subject Line

When a *subject line* is used, it serves as a title to the body of the letter and should be typed a double space below the salutation. In the AMS Simplified letter style, a subject line is used in place of the salutation. (See Illustration 10-9.) The subject line may be typed at the left margin. With the Modified Block letter style (see ¶ 1019), the subject line may be centered, begin at the left margin, or be indented five spaces (similar to the paragraphs) depending upon which paragraph style is used. The words *SUBJECT* or *RE* are sometimes used with the subject line, but are not necessary. The subject line can be typed in capitals, in capitals and lowercase, or in capitals and lowercase underlined. A double space is left below the subject line, above the body of the letter.

```
Detroit, MI  48219-8615

Dear Dr. Stringer:

              ANNUAL PEDIATRICIANS CONFERENCE
```

```
Detroit, MI  48219-8615

Dear Dr. Stringer:

SUBJECT: Annual Pediatricians Conference
```

```
Detroit, MI  48219-8615

Dear Dr. Stringer:

    RE:  Annual Pediatricians Conference
```

1011   Body

The body of the letter carries the message to the reader. The body is single-spaced, with double spacing between paragraphs. Paragraphs begin at the left margin, except for the Modified Block with Indented Paragraphs letter style in which paragraphs may be indented five spaces.

An effort should be made to have at least two paragraphs in a letter. Avoid having paragraphs that are too long or too short. A very short letter can be double-spaced to maintain balance on the page. (See Illustration 10-6.)

ILLUSTRATION 10-6

Very Short, Double-Spaced Letter

Sciotoville
Farm Equipment
P.O. Box 29
Sciotoville, OH 45662-2115

July 12, 19--

Allen Morse Realty
One Biscayne Boulevard
Miami, FL 33132-3572

Ladies and Gentlemen:

One copy of our signed lease agreement arrived today. Thank you for sending it so promptly.

We look forward to our continued business relationships.

Sincerely yours,

Peter J. Masiko, Jr.
President

kss

Quoted material. *Quoted material* within a letter should be preceded by a double space and indented five spaces from each margin unless the quote is less than four lines. Double-space again before continuing with the letter.

Tabulated material. *Tabulated material* is centered within the margins of the letter and indented at least five spaces from each margin, if possible. The use of tabulated information within a letter permits the inclusion of increased amounts of information in a clear and concise manner. (See Illustration 10-8.)

1012   Complimentary Close

A recent survey of businesses found that the majority used "Very truly yours" or "Sincerely." Two other *complimentary closes* used were "Yours very truly" and "Sincerely yours." The complimentary close is typed at the left margin (Block style) or beginning at the center of the page (Modified Block style), a double space below the end of the body of the letter. Only the first letter of the first word is capitalized.

With mixed punctuation, a comma is used after the complimentary close, but with open punctuation, no punctuation follows the close. (See Punctuation Styles, ¶ 1018.)

> Sincerely, (Mixed)   Sincerely (Open)

Note: In the AMS Simplified letter style, the complimentary close is omitted.

1013   Company Name and Signature Lines

Company name. In many companies, the *company name* follows the complimentary close. If used, the company name is typed a double space below the complimentary close in all capital letters. The company name begins exactly at the same horizontal position as the complimentary close.

Signature lines. The *signature lines* refer to those lines naming the letter originator, the originator's title, and/or the originator's department. If a company name is used, the signature lines begin on the fourth line space below the company name. Without the company name, the signature lines begin on the fourth line space below the complimentary close. The signature lines also begin at the same horizontal position as the complimentary close. Examples of different types of signature lines, with and without company names, follow. Also see Illustration 10-3 and other illustrative letters later in this unit.

Sincerely,	Very truly yours
PADRON & AVELLO, INC.	PRIDE INTERNATIONAL
Julio A. Avella	*Loretha Robinson*
Julio A. Avello, Director Public Relations	Loretha Robinson, Ph.D. Dean of Students

Sincerely yours   Sincerely,

[signature: Tomoko Sumida]   *[signature: (Miss) Janice Howard]*

Ms. Tomoko Sumida   For Daniel Morris
Manager   Production Manager

- Titles may be on the same line following the originator's name (separated by a comma) or may be typed on the following line.

- Titles of *Miss, Mrs.*, and *Ms.* may be typed or shown in the signature. Parentheses are optional around such titles.

- "Cordially" and "Cordially yours" are also used occasionally as complimentary closes.

Cordially   Cordially yours,

AMERICAN BAR ASSOCIATION

                                         George B. Livingston
Judge Ellen Morphonias   Secretary to Miss Taylor
Fifth Circuit Court
Alameda County

Hyphenated names. Some *hyphenated names* are representative of two cultures. A hyphenated name such as Hernandez-Fumero is used by a Hispanic male or female. The two names represent the father's and mother's sides of the family. They are both used and hyphenated to indicate a pride in heritage. When a hyphenated Hispanic name is used, the signature will always reflect the same hyphenation.

Yours very truly,

[signature: Mario Hernandez-Fumero]

Mario Hernandez—Fumero
Vice—President for Business

The second practice reflected by *hyphenated last names* is the trend of many married females to use both their maiden and married names. Thus, Miss Bonnie Landsea who married Mr. Jeffrey Schneider would become:

Mrs. Bonnie Landsea—Schneider
Bonnie Landsea—Schneider
Mrs. Jeffrey Landsea—Schneider

This usage also reflects a pride in family heritage. It differs, however, from the Hispanic usage in that the signature often does not reflect the hyphenated name.

Sincerely,   Very truly yours,

Bonnie Schneider   *Bonnie Landsea-Schneider*

Bonnie Landsea–Schneider   Mrs. Bonnie Landsea–Schneider
Project Director   Project Director

Special signatures. Sometimes two individuals write and sign a letter. Suggested format includes space for both signatures. When a name could belong to either a male or a female, efforts should be taken to inform the reader of the proper title for return correspondence.

Sincerely,

Mr. Lynn Forrester   and   Dr. Sheila Long
Professor   Department Chairperson

1014 Reference Initials

Reference initials are typed a double space below the final signature line and at the left margin. These initials identify:

1. *The typist completing the letter*

   jty   kd   MHR

2. *The writer of the letter (first initials) and the typist*

   ALR:kss   TRD/MMJ   SJ:rm

3. *The signer of the letter (first initials), the writer of the letter (second initials), and the typist*

   CHG:MMG:jow   CHG/MMG/jow

Sometimes the writer of the letter (if different from the signer) is indicated in the reference initials as

   LRWhite/pp

1015 Enclosure Notation

When one or more items is to be sent in the envelope with the letter, an *enclosure notation* should be used. The enclosure notation is typed at the left margin, a double space below the reference initials. The following styles are used for enclosure notations:

Enclosure   Enclosures (2)   Check enclosed
Enc.   Enc. 2   2 Enc.
Enclosures:
   1. Check # 778
   2. Invoice #8A

- Some writers use the term *Attachment* or *Att.* for enclosure, especially if any item actually is to be stapled to the letter.

- If material is not being mailed in the envelope with the letter, but sent separately, on the line below the enclosure notation (if any), one of the following styles should be used:

```
Separate mailing 1      In separate mailing:
                        Annual Report
```

1016   Carbon Copy Notation

When carbon copies of the letter are to be sent to other individuals, a *carbon copy notation* should be typed at the left margin, a double space below the enclosure notation.

```
cc Mr. Hyatt      cc Art Department      cc Ms. Judy Adams
   Dr. Marcus     cc Sales Managers         Miss Faye Glover
                                            Mr. David Beemer
```

Also used:

```
CC: Maxine Smith        copy to Purchasing
    Joan Alexander
```

At times it is necessary to send a copy of a letter to someone without the addressee's knowledge. When this occurs, a *blind carbon copy* (bcc) notation is made. Place a 5″ × 3″ card in front of the original. Type as below:

```
bcc: Ms. Jeannette Davies
     Legal Department
```

This notation will now appear on the copy being sent as well as the file copy, but not on the original letter.

When enclosures are to be sent with the letter, it is desirable to indicate whether enclosures accompany the carbon copies. Whether carbon copies are signed or not is really up to the originator; most are not signed. A check mark (√) is usually placed beside the name of the individual receiving each copy before distribution.

```
cc  Mike Griffey (with enclosures)
    Charlotte Gallogly (without enclosures)
√   Jeffrey Williams (without enclosures)
```

1017   Postscript

A postscript can be used effectively to add a new idea, emphasize an old idea, or provide additional information. The postscript is blocked or indented to match the paragraphs in the letter body, a double space below the carbon copy notation. The postscript can be typed alone (see Illustration 10-3) or can be preceded by *P.S.* (or *PS:*).

```
P.S. The date of our ten-year class reunion is April 14,
19--.  Mark your calendar now!
```

PUNCTUATION STYLES

1018   There are two basic styles used in business letters today.

- **Mixed Punctuation:** Most used; colon after salutation; comma after complimentary close

- **Open Punctuation:** No punctuation after salutation or complimentary close

BUSINESS LETTER STYLES

1019   There are four basic letter styles used in the office.

- **Block:** All lines begin at the left margin.

- **Modified Block with Block Paragraphs:** All lines begin at the left margin except the date, complimentary close, and signature lines which should begin at the center of the page.

- **Modified Block with Indented Paragraphs:** Exactly like the first modified block, except that paragraphs are indented five spaces and the subject line may be centered or indented five spaces to match the paragraphs.

- **AMS Simplified:** All lines begin at the left margin. The subject line is substituted for a salutation, and the complimentary close is eliminated.

The illustrative letters that follow contain examples of the four basic business letter styles, as well as other styles used less often. Other examples include correct punctuation and special features of letters.

Special Features	*Illustrated in Letter No.*
• Four-Line Address	10-8; 10-9; 10-11; 10-12; 10-15
• Subject Line	10-9; 10-17
• Unusual Paragraphing	10-10; 10-11; 10-12; 10-13
• Tabulation	10-8; 10-18; 10-19
• Special Display Lines	10-10; 10-13
• Postscript	10-7
• Carbon Copy Notation	10-8
• Mailing Notation	10-8
• Modified Block Style with Mixed Punctuation	10-7
• Block Style with Open Punctuation	10-8
• AMS Simplified Style	10-9
• Direct-Mail Style	10-10
• Inverted Paragraph Style	10-11
• Letter with Side Headings	10-12
• Letter of Application	10-13; 10-15
• Personal Data Sheet	10-14; 10-16
• Two-Page Letter	10-17; 10-18; 10-19; 10-20

ILLUSTRATION 10-7

Modified Block Style; Mixed Punctuation; Postscript

Bay Area MARINE SUPPLY
2232 WATERFRONT DRIVE • SAN FRANCISCO, CA 94123-1178

December 23, 19--

Mr. Robert Samloff
6152 Jensen Street
Wheaton, IL 60187-7290

Dear Mr. Samloff:

I am pleased to confirm May 22 as the delivery date for your new 32-foot "Starbrite" cruiser. The factory representatives assure me that the special options you ordered can be worked into their production schedule without any difficulty.

Our original quotation of $192,500 is now a firm price. It is payable at the time title is transferred.

You have selected a fine boat; I hope you will spend many enjoyable hours aboard.

Very truly yours,

J. D. Arnold, President

jh

As you know, a member of our staff will be available to assist you on a shakedown cruise at your convenience anytime within 60 days of delivery.

ILLUSTRATION 10-8

Block Style; Open Punctuation; Mailing Notation; Carbon Copy Notation

WESTERN TRANSPORT COMPANY
704 MOHAWK DRIVE
BOULDER, CO 80303-8820

April 3, 19--

SPECIAL DELIVERY

Ms. Eugenia Grabowski
Grabowski Manufacturing Co.
705 Amherst Lane
Elmhurst, IL 60126-7369

Dear Ms. Grabowski

Yes, we can supply you regularly with trailer-pulling service and guarantee the-day pickup service. We maintain three major motor pools; the midwest pool, which is located just outside Chicago, would serve you.

Our rates are based on a ton-mile formula: Multiply the number of tons (of cargo only) by the distance hauled to determine the number of ton miles; multiply that answer by our current rate (32 cents per ton mile). The answer is your cost.

The runs you inquired about are listed in the following table:

Run Number	Average Tons	Miles	Ton Mile	Your Cost
1	10	152	1520	486.40
2	8	241	1928	616.96
3	4	20	80	150.00*
4	7	166	1162	371.84
5	6	342	2052	656.64
6	5	288	1440	460.80

*Minimum charge.

We are looking forward to serving you.

Yours very truly

D. L. Myerson
Sales Department

ck

Copy to Rate Department

ILLUSTRATION 10-9
AMS Simplified Style

FAIRVIEW OFFICE EQUIPMENT
7955 N. Third Avenue
Brooklyn, NY 11202-7985

September 12, 19--

Miss Julie Benson
Office Manager
Avilichi, Inc.
1226 Soto Avenue
Orange, CA 92667-9622

OFFICE SUPPLIES

The new era of business correspondence is here! Cleaner letter styles, more attractive letterheads and envelopes, new colored typewriter ribbons that produce a sharper impression, new type faces, postage meters, automatic letter openers--and many other innovations just as important--are available today.

The office manager is usually a busy person who puts off a trip to the stationer's store.

Perhaps you have been ordering the same old items by telephone and missing the chance to learn about all the newest things that are available. I would like to suggest one of two steps that will let you see what is new: that will take only a little of your valuable time.

1. Permit me to call on you, show you some of the new items, and leave a copy of our catalog, or

2. Simply call 262-7844 and have a catalog sent to you.

Either way, you will be opening the door to a new era of eye-pleasing correspondence and economical office appliances which make life in the office world more pleasant!

JERRY PARKS, SALES MANAGER

ch

ILLUSTRATION 10-10
Direct-Mail Style; Mixed Punctuation

HEINER'S Music Company
4200 Lakeshore Drive   Chicago, IL 606/12-2763

January 24, 19--

Dear Parent:

For those who understand and appreciate the finer things in life, the world of music is a delight that can last a lifetime.

Perhaps you yourself play an instrument or enjoy listening to music. Perhaps you have never cared much for music, but you recognize that your children should have an opportunity to enjoy music at an early age.

Heiner's Music provides a variety of instruments and services:

Instruments. Heiner's offers for sale or for rent the most popular brands of stringed, brass, and percussion instruments.

Instruction. Heiner's has a staff of competent instructors who can provide expert guidance at convenient hours.

Music. Heiner's stocks a complete line of orchestrations, sheet music, and instruction books.

Supplies. Heiner's supplies all the incidental supplies necessary to keep your instrument in tip-top playing condition.

Records. Heiner's has a complete selection of record players and records.

Whatever your preference--classical, country and western, jazz, Dixieland, folk, band, orchestra, the newest or the oldest--stop by Heiner's and get your family into the swing of musical things!

Sincerely yours,

HEINER'S MUSIC COMPANY

Carol Eyck

Miss Carol Eyck, Manager

mt

ILLUSTRATION 10-12

Letter with Side Headings; Open Punctuation

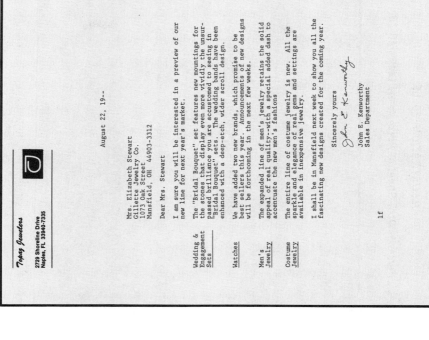

Topaz Jewelers
2729 Shoreline Drive
Naples, FL 33940-7335

August 22, 19--

Mrs. Elizabeth Stewart
Gillette Jewelry Co.
1073 Oak Street
Mansfield, OH 44903-3312

Dear Mrs. Stewart

I am sure you will be interested in a preview of our new line for next year's market.

Wedding & Engagement Sets — The "Bridal Bouquet" set features new mountings for the stones that display even more vividly the unsurpassed brilliance you are accustomed to seeing in "Bridal Bouquet" sets. The wedding bands have been enhanced with a deep-etch, wider scroll design.

Watches — We have added two new brands, which promise to be best sellers this year. Announcements of new designs will be forthcoming in the next few weeks.

Men's Jewelry — The expanded line of men's jewelry retains the solid appeal of real quality--with a special added dash to accentuate the new men's fashions

Costume Jewelry — The entire line of costume jewelry is new. All the sparkle and elegance of real gems and settings are available in inexpensive jewelry.

I shall be in Mansfield next week to show you all the fascinating new designs created for the coming year.

Sincerely yours

John E. Kenworthy

John E. Kenworthy
Sales Department

lf

ILLUSTRATION 10-11

Inverted Paragraph Style; Mixed Punctuation

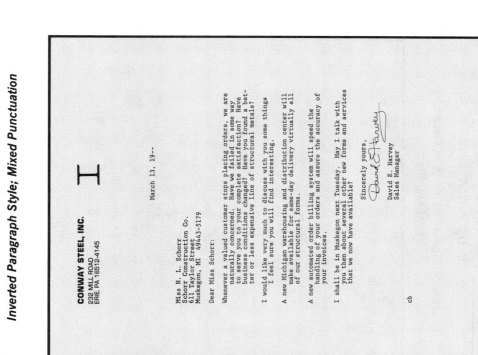

CONWAY STEEL, INC.
232 MILL ROAD
ERIE, PA 16512-4145

March 13, 19--

Miss N. L. Schorr
Schorr Construction Co.
611 Taylor Street
Muskegon, MI 49443-5179

Dear Miss Schorr:

Whenever a valued customer stops placing orders, we are naturally concerned. Have we failed in some way to serve you to your complete satisfaction? Have business conditions changed? Have you found a better or less expensive line of structural metals?

I would like very much to discuss with you some things I feel sure you will find interesting.

A new Michigan warehousing and distribution center will make available for same-day delivery virtually all of our structural forms.

A new automated order billing system will speed the handling of your orders and assure the accuracy of your invoices.

I shall be in Muskegon next Tuesday. May I talk with you then about several other new forms and services that we now have available?

Sincerely yours,

David E. Harvey

David E. Harvey
Sales Manager

cb

ILLUSTRATION 10-13

Letter of Application: Modified Block Style; Mixed Punctuation

```
                                514 West 102 Street
                                Euclid, OH 44123-3143
                                June 3, 19--

Juarez and Allen Company
Attention Mr. Jack O'Brien
3702 Ellis Way
Cleveland, OH 44120-3295

Ladies and Gentlemen

Are you facing that vacation "double-up" inconvenience

  --when the regular staff must assume additional
    responsibilities?
  --when you work overtime yourself to keep routines
    on their daily schedule?
  --when the potential for errors reaches its all-
    season high?

Then you may be interested in knowing that a person is
available

  --who has commercial skills such as stenography,
    typing, filing, use of Dictaphone, bookkeeping.
  --who is adaptable.
  --who enjoys the role of a substitute employee.
  --who does not need to be told twice.
  --who is alert and accurate.
  --who has no designs on a permanent position.

Will you please read the attached personal data sheet
for Linda Jessup to supplement these statements?

Please mark your calendar to call 447-1080 for an inter-
view with an applicant for that summer vacancy.

                              Yours very truly,

                              Linda Jessup

                              Miss Linda Jessup


Enclosure
```

ILLUSTRATION 10-14

Personal Data Sheet to Accompany Letter 10-13

```
                         PERSONAL DATA

                          Linda Jessup
                       514 West 102 Street
                       Euclid, OH  44123-3143

Education:

     Two years, University Extension Division
     One year, Junior College (Evening School)
     Commercial graduate, Southwest High School

Experience:

     Two years as stenographer, Publication Department,
     American Medical Association

     Two years as a case reporting and legal stenographer,
     Richards, Page, and Larkin, Attorneys-at-Law

     Assistant to registrar during junior and senior years
     in high school

References (by permission):

     Mr. Robert Richards
     Suite 1432 Mariner Tower
     Cleveland, OH  44118-3285

     Dr. Mary L. Howes
     American Medical Association
     1631 Abington Road
     Cleveland, OH  44106-3254

     Ms. Yolanda R. Lane, Instructor
     Junior College (Evening School)
     Cleveland, OH  44118-3212

     Mr. Fernando Alvarez
     Southwest High School
     Cleveland, OH  44123-3263
```

ILLUSTRATION 10-15

Letter of Application: Modified Block Style; Open Punctuation

62 Diego Street
San Francisco, CA 94132-9724
July 15, 19--

Pauly Airplane Corporation
Research Department
243 Larkin Street
San Francisco, CA 94102-9735

Ladies and Gentlemen

"Experience in the field of . . . Electronics and Instrumentation." Those qualifications prompt my asking you to consider me for one of the openings at your Aeronautical Research Center.

On the enclosed data sheet I have outlined those of my qualifications that particularly refer to the type of position you have available. In preparing the personal data material, I have attempted to cover all the items listed in your July 12 advertisement in the San Francisco Chronicle.

I shall be glad to come in for an interview at any time that is convenient for you. I shall appreciate the opportunity of discussing my qualifications with you.

A telephone call to 731-1138 will reach me.

Very truly yours

Fred Harvey

cr

Enclosure

ILLUSTRATION 10-16

Personal Data Sheet to Accompany Letter 10-15

PERSONAL DATA SHEET

Fred Harvey

Electronics

Since taking my mechanical engineering degree at the University of California at Los Angeles in 19--, I have completed a two-year Industrial Electronics course in the University's Evening School.

Instrumentation

On the job in the Development Department of the Morse Control Company, San Francisco, I have had four years of design in temperature, pressure, and humidity controls.

During this last year I have applied for three patents in new designs of control elements.

Many of my original designs of pressure and temperature controls are in commercial production.

Personal

I am 30 years old, an American citizen, and single.
My present address is 62 Diego Street, San Francisco, CA 94132-9724.
My telephone number is 731-1138.

Education

San Mateo High School, San Mateo, California, 19-- through 19--.
University of California, Los Angeles, California, 19-- through 19--.
Further technical training includes the equivalent of a four-year machinist's apprenticeship as well as three years in tool design of instrument parts.

Employment

Morse Control Company since May, 19--.

References

My references will be submitted upon request.

ILLUSTRATION 10-17

Two-Page Letter: Subject Line; Quoted Material

Standard

Standard Roofing Co.
454 Van Pelt Street Philadelphia, PA 19103-4767

September 12, 19--

Meyer and Grayson, Architects
5031 Augustine Road
Muncie, IN 47301-4222

Ladies and Gentlemen

Central High School Building

Since the subcontract for roofing on the Central High School project was awarded to us last May, our engineers have reviewed this week the original specifications. We find that several modifications of the specifications would facilitate the work and produce a better roofing job.

Specification 23 now reads in part as follows:

. . . and all other flashing of external fixtures and devices including but not limited to plumbing vents, electrical connections, and utility housings shall be sealed with bituminous roofing compound.

Our experience indicates that the new synthetic rubber sealants are far superior to the older bituminous compounds. The synthetic rubber sealant can be substituted at an increase in cost of only $200.

The original specifications call for three skylights:

    1 Sontage Model 24SLR
    2 Sontage Model 16SLR

Since the Sontage Manufacturing Company no longer markets either of these skylights, substitutions of similar units are indicated. For a well-made unit and prompt delivery, the following skylights are suggested:

    1 Easymount BLO24
    2 Easymount BLO16

The cost of these units would be the same as those originally specified.

Specification 27 calls for the use of Amalgum decorative tile on the mansard roof over the main entrance. Although this material

ILLUSTRATION 10-18

Second Page of Letter 10-17

Meyer and Grayson, Architects
Page 2
September 12, 19--

is attractive and colorful, our experience with previous applications indicates that it tends to fade with exposure to the sun. Perhaps the decorative effect you desire could be achieved by using natural multicolored slate or ribbed copper. If the bright orange color is important, we would recommend the use of anodized aluminum roofing tiles. Cost would be:

    Natural slate $1,022 additional
    Ribbed copper   685 additional
    Anodized aluminum tile   468 additional

The enclosed descriptive material provides pictures and specifications of all materials suggested. Your early response will enable us to order materials at once and assure the completion of our part of the project on schedule.

Sincerely yours

Arthur Crewe

Arthur Crewe
President

cd

Enclosure

ILLUSTRATION 10-19

Two-Page Letter: Subheadings; Tabulations

ILLUSTRATION 10-20

Second Page of Letter 10-19

Trendco

TRENDCO RENTAL, INC.
Box 75
Santa Barbara, CA 93108-7690

November 2, 19--

Dr. Ken Stringer
115 Horizon Avenue
Chicago, IL 60624-5926

Dear Dr. Stringer:

It was a pleasure to discuss with you the advantages of the TRENDCO RENTAL franchise plan. I was particularly pleased to receive your follow-up letter. The franchise plan has proven successful in many businesses. The TRENDCO RENTAL plan has already been employed successfully in many cities, and there is every reason to believe that one or more TRENDCO RENTAL stores would thrive in Chicago.

Service to Contractors. The TRENDCO RENTAL plan makes available to large and small construction firms the equipment they need occasionally but cannot economically own and maintain themselves. Typical units stocked for the construction industry are as follows:

Concrete saws	Concrete breakers
Ditch diggers	Power rollers
Jack hammers	Concrete grinders
Power shovels	Sandblasters
Air compressors	Jumping jacks

Service to Homeowners. For the do-it-yourself homeowner, the TRENDCO RENTAL plan makes available tools that are needed only occasionally. Typical tools stocked for the do-it-yourself trade are as follows:

Rototillers	Circular saws
Mowers	Wheelbarrows
Edgers	Sewer cleaners
Seeders	Drills
Sprayers	Grinders
Lawn vacuums	Wallpaper steamers
Chain saws	Rug scrubbers
Log splitters	Floor polishers

TRENDCO RENTAL Franchise Service. The unique services of TRENDCO RENTAL make operation of a tool-rental business a smooth and profitable occupation. The intercity pool makes available to

---

Dr. Ken Stringer   2   November 2, 19--

you and to your customer seldom-used tools from other franchise holders. Normally, any tool you need is available within 48 hours.

The promotion package offers advertising material developed by experts to promote your business in your city. The local advertising package, of course, ties in with the national advertising program.

The accounting package provides a ready-made system of inventory control, cash control, billing, and statement preparation. The preparation of financial statements and tax returns is part of the service.

The attractive, functional, prefabricated building package provides the best in physical facilities without duplication of planning effort and in the shortest possible time.

The TRENDCO RENTAL team of experts is available to each new franchise owner for as long as it is needed to establish every new store.

Please study the enclosed booklet carefully and let us hear from you when you are ready to enter the profitable world of TRENDCO RENTAL franchise owners!

Sincerely yours,

Joan Anderson

Joan Anderson, President

es
Enclosure

1020   Second Pages

When a letter is longer than one page, all additional pages should be on *plain paper* of the same quality as the letterhead used for the first sheet. Use the same left and right margins on all pages. Two popular methods are used for headings when a letter extends to more than one page. These begin on line seven of the page (leaving a one-inch top margin). See example in Illustrations 10-18 and 10-20.

```
Meyer and Grayson, Architects
Page 2
September 12, 19--
```

                              or

```
Meyer and Grayson, Architects    2    September 12, 19--
```

After typing the second page heading, triple-space and continue the message of the letter. There are, however, some guidelines for determining exactly where to break for an additional page within a business letter:

- Do not divide a paragraph between pages unless you leave at least two lines on the preceding page and carry over at least two lines to the following page.

- Do not use a second page to type only the complimentary close, signature lines, and closing notations. At least two lines of the final paragraph should accompany this information on a final letter page.

- Try to leave a uniform margin of at least one inch at the bottom of the second and all subsequent letter pages, except for the last page which may have a larger bottom margin.

- Do not divide the final word on a page.

CARBON COPIES

1021   The type of paper on which carbon copies are typed, usually called *second sheets*, varies from company to company. Some companies have special sheets with a simplified letterhead for carbon copies going outside of the company. Colored sheets are also used for carbon copy file copies. Some lightweight second sheets simply have the word *copy* imprinted on the top. Determine the preferences of the office in which you work. If there are no specific preferences, choose second-sheet stationery with the aid of your local office supply store, taking into consideration the average number of copies required.

The choice of *carbon paper* is also dependent on the number of copies you are required to type. Carbon paper is available in hard, medium, and soft finishes; the hard finish produces the clearest copy, but the softest finish produces the largest number of copies.

"Snap out" carbon packs are available. In these packs, the carbon paper is already connected to a second sheet, and the second sheets are available in a choice of colors.

When typing multiple carbon copies, it is necessary to assemble the carbon pack quickly and efficiently. Three methods of assembling carbon packs are commonly used: (1) the desk assembly method, (2) the machine assembly method, and (3) the slotted desk drawer assembly method.

Desk assembly method. The *desk assembly method* requires a flat desk surface. Place one second sheet down first; add a sheet of carbon paper with the carbon side down (against the second sheet); continue alternating in this manner, including a carbon sheet and a second sheet for each copy required. At the very top of the carbon pack, place your original with the letterhead facing up.

To insert the carbon pack, pick up the entire set of papers including the letterhead. Holding loosely, tap the edges against the desk until the top and left edges are even. The ends of the carbon paper should extend beyond the bottom of the letterhead and second sheets. Holding the carbon pack so that the carbon side of the carbon paper is facing you, roll the entire pack into your typewriter. Sometimes the carbon pack will roll more easily into the typewriter if you place the entire pack under the flap of an envelope and roll the envelope into the typewriter. Remove the envelope once the carbon pack is inserted into the machine.

After inserting the carbon pack, operate the paper release to smooth out possible wrinkles in the carbon paper which would cause marks on the second sheets. Also realign the entire pack in the machine, taking care to make certain it is straight and the top edges of all sheets are aligned. Finally, make sure that as you roll the carbon pack into the machine, the original is facing you and the uncarbon side is toward you.

Machine assembly method. In the machine assembly method of assembling a carbon pack, follow these steps:

1. Arrange a stack of white sheets (with the original on top) for insertion into the typewriter.

2. Insert the sheets until the tops are gripped slightly by the feed rolls; then lay all but the last sheet over the top of the machine.

3. Place carbon sheets between the sheets of paper with the carbon sides toward you. Flip each sheet back as you add each carbon.

4. Roll the pack into typing position.

5. After the typing is completed, remove the carbon sheets. Since the carbon sheets do not extend to the top edge of the paper, it is easy to remove all the sheets at one time by pulling them out as you hold the left top edge of the paper.

Slotted desk drawer assembly method. In the slotted desk drawer assembly method of assembling a carbon pack, the secretary utilizes the arrangement of the stationery supplies in a slotted desk drawer. The letterheads should be kept in the slot at the extreme left; the carbon sheets should be kept in the next slot to the right; the second sheets should be kept in the third slot. With this arrangement, follow these steps:

1. Pick up a letterhead with your left hand and a sheet of carbon paper with your right hand. Pull the sheets slightly forward, then grasp both sheets with your left hand as you reach with your right hand to pull the second sheet into position.

2. Pull the sheets from the slots.

3. Straighten the pack by tapping it gently on the desk as you hold the sides of the sheets loosely by both hands.

4. Add a second sheet and a carbon for any additional copies that you need.

5. Insert the pack into the typewriter in the usual manner.

SPECIAL SALUTATIONS

1022   Salutations for more than one person, for persons of unknown sex, and for persons whose position or rank requires a specialized salutation are included in this section.

One Person, Sex Unknown

Dear Lynn Forrester: Dear F. G. Harrison:

One Person, Name Unknown, Sex Unknown

Dear Sir or Madam:

One Woman, Title Preference Unknown

Dear Ms. Streit: or   Dear Anita Streit:

Two or More Men

Dear Mr. Issacson and Mr. Polansky:
Dear Messrs. Issacson and Polansky:

Two or More Women

Dear Ms. Gonzalez, Mrs. Cordova, and Miss Gettings

* if both married

    Dear Mrs. Gorden and Mrs. Bryant:
    Dear Mesdames Gorden and Bryant:

* if both unmarried

    Dear Miss Gorden and Miss Bryant:
    Dear Misses Gorden and Bryant:

* if both use Ms.

    Dear Ms. Gorden and Ms. Bryant:
    Dear Mses. (or Mss.) Gorden and Bryant:

A Woman and a Man

Dear Ms. Gorden and Mr. Issacson:

Several Persons

Dear Ms. Gorden, Mrs. Bryant, Mr. Issacson, and Mr. Polansky:
Dear Neighbors (Colleagues, Friends, Professors, etc.):

An Organization Composed Entirely of Women

Ladies: or   Mesdames:

An Organization Composed Entirely of Men

Gentlemen:

An Organization Composed of Women and Men

Ladies and Gentlemen:

Salutations for government officials, members of the clergy, members of the armed services, and educational officials are included below. Some forms of address have been shown with masculine titles and others with feminine titles. To convert any title to the opposite sex, simply reverse:

Madam—Sir
Mr.—Miss, Mrs., or Ms.
Madam (with title)—Mr. (with title)

TITLE AND BEGINNING LINES OF INSIDE ADDRESS

SALUTATION

Alderman

Alderman (full name)	Dear Alderman (surname)
Alderwoman (full name)	Dear Alderwoman (surname)
The Honorable (full name)	Dear Mr. (surname)
Alderman, City of _____	Dear Ms., Mrs., Miss (surname)

Ambassador

The Honorable (full name)
Ambassador of the United States

Dear Ambassador (surname)
Dear Mr. Ambassador
Dear Madam Ambassador

The Honorable (full name)
Ambassador to the United Nations

Archbishop

The Most Reverend
Archbishop of (diocese)

Your Excellency
Dear Archbishop (surname)

Armed Forces

Captain (full name), USCG
Colonel (full name), USAF
General (full name), USMC
Admiral (full name), USN
General (full name), USA
Sergeant (full name), USA
Seaman (full name), USN

Dear (rank) (surname)

Associate Justice of the Supreme Court

Ms., Mrs., Miss Justice (surname)
Mr. Justice (surname)
The Supreme Court of the
    United States

Dear Madam Justice
Dear Mr. Justice
Dear Mr. Justice (surname)
Dear Madam Justice (surname)

Bishop (Catholic)

The Most Reverend (surname)
Bishop of (diocese)

Your Excellency
Dear Bishop (surname)

Bishop (Protestant)

The Reverend (full name)   Dear Bishop (surname)
Bishop of _____   Dear Mr. (surname)
                                  Dear Ms., Mrs. Miss (surname)
The Right Reverend (surname)

Brother

Brother (surname)   Dear Brother
_____ Seminary   Dear Brother (surname)

Cabinet Member

The Honorable (full name)   Dear Madam Secretary
Secretary of (department name)   Dear Mr. Secretary
                                  Dear Secretary (surname)

Cardinal (Catholic)

His Eminence, (given name),   Your Eminence
    Cardinal (surname)   Dear Cardinal (surname)
Archbishop of (diocese)

Chief Justice of the Supreme Court

The Chief Justice   Dear Mr. Chief Justice
The Supreme Court   Dear Madam Chief Justice

The Honorable (full name)
Chief Justice of the United States

City Attorney

Honorable (full name)   Dear City Attorney (surname)
City Attorney

Commissioner, Director, or Chief of the Government Bureau

The Honorable (full name)   Dear Ms., Mrs., Miss (surname)
(Commissioner, Director, or Chief) Dear Mr. (surname)
(name of government bureau)

Consul

Mr. (full name)   Dear Mr. (surname)
Ms., Mrs., Miss (full name)   Dear Ms., Mrs., Miss (surname)
United States Consul

Council Member

Council Member (full name)   Dear Council Member (surname)

The Honorable (full name)   Dear Mr. (surname)
Council Member, City of _____   Dear Ms., Mrs., Miss (surname)

County Officials

Honorable (full name)   Dear Ms., Mrs., Miss (surname)
Supervisor, (county)   Dear Mr. (surname)
                                       Dear Supervisor (surname)

Dean of a School

Dean (full name)   Dear Dean (surname)
College of (name)

Dr. (full name)   Dear Dr. (surname)
Associate Dean

District Attorney

The Honorable (full name)   Dear District Attorney
District Attorney   (surname)
County Courthouse   Dear Ms., Mrs., Miss (surname)
                                       Dear Mr. (surname)

Foreign Officials

Her excellency (surname)   Excellency
His excellency (surname)   Dear Ambassador (surname)
Ambassador of (country)

Minister of (country)

Governor

The Honorable (full name)   Dear Governor (surname)
Governor of (state)

Judge

The Honorable (full name)   Dear Judge (surname)
Judge of the (name of court)

Lieutenant Governor

The Honorable (full name)   Dear Lieutenant Governor
Lieutenant Governor of (state)   (surname)

Mayor

The Honorable (full name)   Dear Mayor (surname)
Mayor of (city)

Member of the Board of Education

Ms., Mrs., Miss (full name)
Mr. (full name)
Member (city) Board of
  Education

Dear Ms., Mrs., Miss (surname)
Dear Mr. (surname)
Dear Board Member (surname)

Minister

The Reverend (full name)
(name of church)

Dear Reverend (surname)
Dear Mr. (surname)
Dear Ms., Mrs., Miss (surname)

Monsignor

The Right Reverend (full name)
(name of church)

Dear Monsignor (surname)

Mother Superior

The Reverend Mother Superior
(church or order)

Reverend Mother
Dear Reverend Mother

Physician

(full name), M.D.

Dr. (full name)

Dear Dr. (surname)

Pope

His Holiness
Vatican City

Pope (full name)

Your Holiness
Most Holy Father

President of a Catholic College

The Very Reverend (full name)
(name of college)

Dear Father (surname)
Dear Mother (surname)

President of a College or University

President (full name)
(name of college or university)

Dear President (surname)
Dear Dr. (surname)

President of the United States

The President
The White House

Dear Mr. President
Dear Madam President
Dear President (surname)

Priest

The Reverend (full name)   Dear Father (surname)
(name of church)

The Reverend (full name), Ph.D.   Dear Dr. (surname)
(name of college or university)

Principal

Dr. (full name), Principal   Dear Dr. (surname)
(name of school)

Principal (full name)   Dear Principal (surname)
(name of school)

Professor

Professor (full name)   Dear Professor (surname)
(department)
(name of school)

Dr. (full name), (title)   Dear Dr. (surname)
(department)
(name of school)

Rabbi

Rabbi (full name)   Dear Rabbi (surname)
(temple name)

Dr. (full name)   Dear Dr. (surname)

Representative (Congressional)

The Honorable (full name)   Dear Representative (surname)
House of Representatives

*Secretary or Assistant to the
President of the United States*

The Honorable (full name)   Dear Madam (surname)
Secretary to the President   Dear Mr. (surname)

Senator

The Honorable (full name)   Dear Senator (surname)
United States Senate

Sister

Sister (full name or religious   Dear Sister (full name or
    name)   religious name)
(order)

Speaker of the House

The Honorable (full name)   Dear Madam Speaker
Speaker of the House of   Dear Mr. Speaker
    Representatives

State Legislators

The Honorable (full name)   Dear Representative (surname)
House of Representatives   Dear Senator (surname)
        or
The State Assembly

State Officials

The Honorable (full name)   Dear Mr. Attorney General
Attorney General of (state)   Dear Madam Attorney General
                                        Dear Attorney General (surname)

United Nations

Her Excellency (full name)   Dear Secretary-General (surname)
His Excellency (full name)   Dear Madam Secretary-General
Secretary-General of the   Dear Mr. Secretary-General
    United Nations

Vice-President of the United States

The Vice-President   Dear Madam Vice-President
United States Senate   Dear Mr. Vice-President
                                        Dear Vice-President (surname)
The Honorable (full name)
Vice-President of the United
    States

SPECIAL-SIZED STATIONERY

1023   Standard-sized stationery measures 8½ by 11 inches. Two
other types of stationery are also used in business offices:

		Margins	*Date on Line*
Monarch	7¼" × 10½"	1"	14
Baronial	5½" × 8½"	½" − ¾"	12

To determine margin settings, first find the center of the page.
Subtract half of the space line from the center for the left margin;
add half of the space line to the center for the right margin.

where the paper begins + where the paper ends ÷ 2 = center

MEMORANDUMS

1024   *Interoffice memorandums,* or *memos*, are basically letters between company employees. At times, carbon copies of such memorandums are sent to nonemployees. Check the policies and procedures used at your office. Memorandums are similar to business letters in many ways. Differences you need to know in memo preparation follow:

- **Printed Memorandum Forms.** Many offices use preprinted memorandum forms in either full or half sheets. In using these forms, align the *to, from, date,* and *subject* information two spaces to the right of the headings. Usually, on these preprinted forms, the left margin will begin even with the name of the addressee. (See Illustration 10-21.)

- **Heading Information.** The *to* and *from* lines should contain both the name and the department of the individuals listed. The *date* line is usually typed similarly to that in a business letter— January 11, 19—; but it is also correct as 1/11—. Capitalization of the *subject* line is optional.

- **Closing Information.** There are no complimentary close or signature lines in a memorandum. The originator usually initials or signs near the name at the top of the page. Reference initials, enclosure notations, carbon copy notations, etc., remain the same as in business letters.

- **No Printed Form.** Without a printed memorandum form, the typist can prepare a memorandum as shown in Illustration 10-22. Note the change in the left margin for balance.

COMPOSITION OF BUSINESS LETTERS AND MEMORANDUMS

1025   The typist should become familiar with typical answers to business correspondence, whether by letter or memorandum. Many offices use form letters of prepared answers to typical office situations which the typist can use to answer routine daily correspondence. The typist can put together examples of some of the most effective paragraphs in past correspondence as a guide in composition of daily answers.

In beginning to develop your composition skills, start with a simple piece of correspondence. Make an outline of all the points you want to make in the answer; i.e., thank you for the order, all products on hand, shipment expected via UPS within the week, look forward to continued business relationship. Next, write a rough draft from the outline. If possible, review your rough draft with other office personnel. Type a final copy. Additional skills can be gained through business communications courses available through your local education programs.

ILLUSTRATION 10-21

Memorandum on a Preprinted Form

Schuster & Schuster
ATTORNEYS-AT-LAW

MEMORANDUM

TO: Ms. Caridad Bombalier, Purchasing Department

FROM: Dr. Josephina Perez, Research Department

DATE: July 12, 19--

SUBJECT: EMPLOYEE PICNIC

Thank you for agreeing to serve on our committee to organize the employee picnic next month. With the group of individuals who will be working on the arrangements, I am sure our picnic this year will be the best ever!

Enclosed with this letter are the following from last year's efforts:

Planning Committee Report
Picnic Budget
Picnic Employee Flyer
Picnic Program
Picnic Evaluation

The first meeting of our planning committee will be in the executive dining room, on Tuesday, July 17, 19--, at 2:00 p.m. My secretary will be calling you to confirm your attendance at this meeting.

Bring all of your best ideas--let's make this picnic one that will be long remembered.

rls

Enclosures

cc Dr. Jack Kassawitz

ILLUSTRATION 10-22

Memorandum Without a Preprinted Form

M E M O R A N D U M

TO: Ms. Caridad Bombalier
     Purchasing Department

FROM: Dr. Josephina Perez
       Research Department

DATE: July 12, 19--

SUBJECT: Employee Picnic

Thank you for agreeing to serve on our committee to organize the employee picnic next month. With the group of individuals who will be working on the arrangements, I am sure our picnic this year will be the best ever!

Enclosed with this letter are the following from last year's efforts:

Planning Committee Report
Picnic Budget
Picnic Employee Flyer
Picnic Program
Picnic Evaluation

The first meeting of our planning committee will be in the executive dining room, on Tuesday, July 17, 19--, at 2:00 p.m. My secretary will be calling you to confirm your attendance at this meeting.

Bring all of your best ideas--let's make this picnic one that will be long remembered.

rls

Enclosures

cc Dr. Jack Kassawitz

UNIT 11
Reports · Manuscripts

Business reports are written to convey information in a clear, concise manner. They may be formal or informal—but should always retain their clarity and conciseness. You probably know something about writing reports because you probably have written reports or manuscripts, or both, as part of your job or as a class assignment.

FORMAL REPORTS

1101   *Formal reports* can contain many parts. Some components are necessary; others are optional.

Business Report

Required	*Optional*
Title Page or Letter of Transmittal	Both the Title Page *and* Letter of Transmittal
Body of Report	Preface/Forward
	Acknowledgments/Dedication
	Table of Contents
	List of Tables
	Bibliography
	Appendix
	Footnotes

Each of the parts is discussed in detail and an example is provided of several of the parts.

1102 Report/Manuscript Spacing

When reports or manuscripts are lengthy, they should be bound in some form. When a staple is simply inserted in the top left-hand corner, the report is said to be *unbound*. When the report is bound (either with staples, spiral, or binding) at the left side, the report is *left bound*. If the binding is at the top, it is a *top-bound* report. Table 11-1 provides the margins for all parts of a business report.

1103   Title Page

The *title page* contains the report title, the writer's name (also title and department on a business report), and the date the report is submitted. Each item is centered horizontally across the page; the title is typed in capitals, with all capitals for the other lines optional. Vertical spacing is chosen for balance of the entire page. (See Illustration 11-1.) However, if the title page is to be bound in a left-bound report, one-half inch should be added to the left margin before horizontally centering each line. With a top-bound report, an extra four to six blank lines should be left at the top of the title page.

ILLUSTRATION 11-1   *Sample Title Page*

```
                    THE CHANGING STUDENT PROFILE




                                by

                          Carol Stevenson
                     Bayside Community College
                          Central Campus




                          July 12, 19--
```

11

TABLE 11-1

Business Report Margins

Type of Page	Unbound					Left Bound					Top Bound				
	Top	Btm.****	Left	Right	Page***	Top	Btm.	Left	Right	Page***	Top	Btm.	Left	Right	Page***
Title Page	*N/A				None	N/A				None	N/A				None
Letter of Transmittal	N/A				btm.	N/A				btm.	N/A				btm.
Preface/Forward	**1½ (Elite: 2)	1	1	1	btm.	1½ (Elite: 2)	1	1½	1	btm.	2	1	1	1	btm.
Acknowledgements/ Dedication	1½ (Elite: 2)	1	1	1	btm.	1½ (Elite: 2)	1	1½	1	btm.	2	1	1	1	btm.
Table of Contents	1½ (Elite: 2)	1	1	1	btm.	1½ (Elite: 2)	1	1½	1	btm.	2	1	1	1	btm.
List of Tables	1½ (Elite: 2)	1	1	1	btm.	1½ (Elite: 2)	1	1½	1	btm.	2	1	1	1	btm.
Body of Report First Page or Major Page Divisions	1½ (Elite: 2)	1	1	1	None	1½ (Elite: 2)	1	1½	1	None	2 (Elite: 2½)	1	1	1	None
All Other Pages	1	1	1	1	top	1	1	1½	1	top	1½	1	1	1	btm.
Bibliography/ Appendix First Page	1½ (Elite: 2)	1	1	1	None	1½ (Elite: 2)	1	1½	1	None	2 (Elite: 2½)	1	1	1	None
All Other Pages	1	1	1	1	top	1	1	1½	1	top	1½	1	1	1	btm.

* N/A = Not Applicable   ** Inches   *** L. 4 = Line 4: top, at right margin; bottom, at center.

1104 Letter of Transmittal

The *letter of transmittal* introduces the report to the intended reader. It can be used to summarize important information, point out certain comparisons, etc. Typing instructions for the letter of transmittal are the same as those for any business letter (see Unit 10). However, if a letter of transmittal is to be bound in a left-bound report, one-half inch should be added to the left margin of the letter; with a top-bound report, begin the dateline four to six lines lower on the page. (See Illustration 11-2.)

1105 Preface/Foreword; Acknowledgements/Dedication (Preceding Lengthy Reports)

The *preface* or *foreword* is a personal message from the author to the reader, sometimes providing special information on methods used in gathering information for the report, and sometimes pointing out special parts of the report itself.

The *acknowledgements* or *dedication* page is another personal message from the author—this time to individuals who have provided special assistance or to whom the volume is dedicated. (See Illustration 11-3.)

As Table 11-1 indicates, the margins for both of these pages are identical. As seen in Illustration 11-3, a triple space follows the title, preceding the first paragraph. The remainder of the page is double-spaced with five-space paragraph indentions.

1106 Table of Contents

A *table of contents* lists each major division in a report and the page number of the first page of that section. The table of contents is not required; when a report is lengthy, it serves to organize the information presented. The margins for both the table of contents and the list of tables are indicated in Table 11-1. A double space follows the title and each major division, with single-spacing within subdivisions. (See Illustration 11-4.)

1107 List of Tables

The *list of tables* is similar to the table of contents, except that it provides a listing of all tables contained within a report. Naturally, you would not have a list of tables unless there were several tables presented within the report. The spacing of the list of tables follows exactly that used for the table of contents. (See Illustration 11-5.)

BODY OF REPORT

The *body of the report* is where the facts and figures of the report are found. There are several steps that can aid you in improving your report composition skills. They begin with an outline.

ILLUSTRATION 11-2   Sample Letter of Transmittal

Bayside Community College
Central Campus
390 W. Tenth Street • Oakland, CA 94320-3990

July 12, 19--

Mr. John Neely, Editor
THE TEACHER'S AID
Central Publishing Co.
1633 Western Avenue
Montrose, CA 92174-7293

Dear Mr. Neely:

Enclosed is an article entitled "The Changing Student Profile" for your consideration for possible publication in THE TEACHER'S AID. This article discusses changes in the business education classrooms of the high school, community college, and university.

This topic is timely for today's educators as they attempt to meet the needs of classrooms full of students with varied abilities. Reasons for increasing and decreasing enrollments, coupled with the effects of these changes on the classroom, are presented with a discussion of possible solutions.

Your Publication Committee's review of my article is most appreciated. I look forward to hearing from you.

Sincerely,

Carol Stevenson

Dr. Carol Stevenson
Associate Dean

mos

Enclosure

ILLUSTRATION 11-3   Sample Dedication Page

DEDICATION

To students--those whom we have the privilege of teaching, from whom we learn much more than we teach, and with whom we keep searching.

ILLUSTRATION 11-5   Sample List of Tables

LIST OF TABLES

ILLUSTRATION 11-4   Sample Table of Contents

TABLE OF CONTENTS

1108 Outline

Just as the journey from one city to another is easier with a road map, the composition of a report is easier when you have an *outline* to follow. Following the outline format in Illustration 11-6, jot down ideas that will help you provide information on:

- *The problem*—On what is the report to focus? State the problem briefly.

- *Background*—What situations have led to identification of this problem? Briefly, provide background information.

- *Procedures*—What procedures were used to gather the information presented in this report? What people were involved in the preparation?

- *Results*—What are the facts and figures on the situations analyzed? What have comparisons shown? What events have occurred?

- *Recommendations*—How can we use the results to make changes that will benefit the organization? What should we do differently with the knowledge we now have? What should we do in the same way?

If possible, share your outline with your colleagues. Share ideas to expand on your original outline. Compare your outline to reports previously submitted in your organization.

With your outline before you, write your first draft of the report.

1109 Body of Report

The *body of the report* is typed in what is called *manuscript style* because it is easy to read. Margins for the first page and subsequent pages are indicated in Table 11-1. Illustration 11-7 shows the first page of the body of the report.

Double-space between the chapter reference and the title; triple-space after the title. First- and second-level subtitles are preceded by a triple space. Double-space in the remainder of the body.

Each paragraph need not have a separate subtitle. Subtitles are used to provide the reader with additional information and clarification. Subtitles can be used to provoke interest in the subject matter being discussed in the following paragraphs.

See Illustration 11-8 for quoted material within a report. When *quoted material* is lengthy, it is sometimes single-spaced. All quoted material of more than three lines is indented five spaces from the left and right margins, with a double space preceding and following the quotation.

ILLUSTRATION 11-6

Possible Outline Organization

```
                    OUTLINE TITLE

I.  MAIN SECTIONS ALL IN CAPITALS
    A.  All Remaining Lines--Capitalize Only First
        Letter of Important Words
        1.  -----------------------------------
        2.  -----------------------------------
            a.  xxxxxxxxxxxxxxxxxxxxxxxxxxxxxxxx
            b.  xxxxxxxxxxxxxxxxxxxxxxxxxxxxxxxx
                (1) -----------------------------
                (2) -----------------------------
                    (a) xxxxxxxxxxxxxxxxxxxxxxxxx
                    (b) xxxxxxxxxxxxxxxxxxxxxxxxx
                        1) --------------------
                        2) --------------------
                            a)  xxxxxxxxxxxxxxxx
                            b)  xxxxxxxxxxxxxxxx
    B.  -------------------------------------

II. SECOND MAIN SECTION
```

ILLUSTRATION 11-7

First Page and Possible Headings, Unbound Report

```
                    CHAPTER I
                  CHAPTER TITLE

    The main heading (usually a chapter or division heading) be-
gins on line 10 (13 top bound) with "CHAPTER" and the number.  A
double space after this is the chapter title: both lines are cen-
tered and typed all in capitals.  The first paragraph begins a
triple space after the heading.

                First-Order Subtitle

    A first-order subtitle is placed a triple space after the
preceding paragraph and centered.  Only the first letter of each
important word is capitalized.  The paragraph begins a double space
after the subtitle.

Second-Order Subtitle

    A second-order subtitle begins a triple space after the pre-
ceding paragraph and is typed at the left margin.  Only the first
letter of each important word is capitalized, but the entire sub-
title is underlined.  The paragraph begins a double space after the
heading and is indented five spaces.

    Third-order subtitle.  A third-order subtitle begins a double
space after the preceding paragraph.  It appears in the position
of a paragraph indention.  The first letter is capitalized, and the
entire subtitle is underlined.  Begin the text on the same line.
```

An example of *listed material* within a report is also shown in Illustration 11-8. Listed material is also indented five spaces from both margins.

Refer to Unit 9 for additional information on polishing your final report through the use of proofreading.

1110   Bibliography

The *bibliography* identifies all sources used, quoted, or paraphrased within the report. Spacing for both the bibliography and appendix pages is identified in Table 11-1.

A triple space follows the title, with single spacing used within each bibliography item and double spacing between items. While the first line of each notation begins at the left margin, subsequent lines are indented five spaces. (See Illustration 11-9.)

Sometimes special forms are used when citing the name of the author or authors in bibliography entries. When there are more than three authors of a single work, the name of the first author is given, followed by the phrase *et al.* ("and others"). When two or more works by the same author are listed, repetition of the author's name is unnecessary. Instead, a line five spaces long, followed by a period, is substituted. Examples of these and other bibliographical forms are found in ¶ 1113.

1111   Appendix

The *appendix* is a consolidation of examples, charts, graphs, memoranda, etc., to further support the recommendations made in the report. Each appendix item may be different in format, depending on the type of information included. As much as possible, however, format should follow that recommended for the bibliography.

1112   Footnotes

Footnotes are references used to cite for the reader the source of any quoted or paraphrased material. An example of traditional footnotes is included in Illustration 11-8. Traditional footnotes are typed beginning with a single space following the last line of manuscript material. The secret to typing footnotes is knowing how much space to leave to type them between the manuscript material and the one inch margin at the bottom of the page. Following the single space, at the left margin, an underline is typed one and one-half inches long. A double space follows, and then the first footnote of the page is indented five spaces and typed single-spaced. Between two footnotes, there is double spacing. Footnote numerical references ([1]) are raised when typed following the quoted material and in the reference at the bottom of the page.

ILLUSTRATION 11-8
Sample Manuscript Page, Top Bound Report

same time span will undoubtedly provide the greatest challenge ever with students entering classrooms with maximum diversity of skills and abilities.

American higher education has worked hard for the past quarter of a century to achieve educational opportunity for all. It looks very much as though we shall spend the remaining 25 years of this century working to achieve education for each. The problems of attaining even minimal educational opportunities for everyone have been so consuming that we have not yet turned full attention to the greater challenge of designing educational experiences that will provide maximum learning for individuals. We have not yet demonstrated that we can deliver an education that is attractive and useful to the majority of Americans.[6]

Patricia Cross stresses the need for improvement in education:

In his new book, Human Characteristics and School Learning, Benjamin Bloom discusses a theory of school learning which can account for most of the variation in school learning under a great variety of conditions. Simply stated, this theory consists of the following:

1. Cognitive entry behaviors. The availability to the learner of requisite entry behavior determines the extent to which a specific task can be learned.

2. Affective entry characteristics. Affective entry characteristics determine the conditions under which the learner will engage in a learning task. [7]

[6] Patricia Cross, "Accent on Learning: Beyond Education for All--Toward Education for Each" (Paper presented at the meeting of the Symposium on Individualized Instruction, Gainesville, April 8, 1976), pp. 21-23.

[7] Benjamin S. Bloom, Human Characteristics and School Learning (New York: McGraw-Hill Book Co., 1976), p. 108.

8

ILLUSTRATION 11-9
Sample Bibliography Page

BIBLIOGRAPHY

Abdullah, Khalid Amin. "A General Survey of Shorthand Teaching Devices." Masters thesis, Texas Technological College. 1966.

Anderson, Ruth I. "An Analysis and Classification of Research in Shorthand and Transcription." Doctoral dissertation, Indiana University, 1946.

_____. "Studying Shorthand--Reading vs. Writing." Business Education World (September, 1948), p. 21.

_____. "Significant Implications of Research in Shorthand and Transcription. Secretarial Education with a Future, 19th Yearbook of the EBTA and NBTA. Somerville, N.J.: EBTA and NBTA, 1962. p. 39.

_____. "Utilizing Shorthand Research in the Classroom." National Business Education Quarterly (March, 1968). pp. 48-49.

_____. "Methods of Instruction in First-Year Shorthand." Effective Secretarial Education. Reston, Va.: NBEA, 1974, pp. 31-45.

Arnold, Boyd Eugene. "The Effects of Combining Shorthand Plates and Printed Materials as Out-of-Class Writing Assignments in First-Semester College Gregg Shorthand." Doctoral dissertation, Pennsylvania State University (University Park), 1974.

Askew, Gloria H. "Structured Shorthand Sparks Student Interest and Learning." Business Education Forum (October, 1974), pp. 11-12.

Audiovisual Aids for Business, Economic, and Distributive Education. Monograph 92. Cincinnati: South-Western Publishing Co., 1972.

Baggett, Harry W., Jr. "The Validity of a Measure of the Difficulty of Gregg Shorthand Dictation Materials." Doctoral dissertation, University of Minnesota, 1964.

Bobbit, Franklin. How to Make a Curriculum. Boston: Houghton-Mifflin Company, 1924.

Hall, Lawrence, et al. New Colleges for New Students. San Francisco: Jossey-Bass Inc., Publishers, 1974.

Klausmeier, Herbert J., and William Goodwin. Learning and Human Abilities. New York: Harper & Row, Publishers, 1966.

Lambrecht, Judith J. "Aptitude Testing in Shorthand." Business Education Forum (October, 1972), pp. 17-24.

BIBLIOGRAPHICAL FORMAT

1113   **Book—One Author**

Bobbit, Franklin. How to Make a Curriculum. Boston:
    Houghton—Mifflin Company, 1924.

Book—Repeating Author

_____. Curriculum and Instruction. Boston:
    Houghton—Mifflin Company, 1926.

Book—Two Authors

Klausmeier, Herbert J., and William Goodwin. Learning and
    Human Abilities. New York: Harper & Row, Publishers,
    1966.

Book—More Than Three Authors

Hall, Lawrence, et al. New Colleges for New Students. San
    Francisco: Jossey—Bass Inc., Publishers, 1974.

Book—with Editor

Skinner, Charles E. (ed.). Educational Psychology. New York:
    Prentice—Hall, 1951.

Book—Chapter Reference

Pullis, Joe M. "Variables Affecting Achievement in Shorthand
    and Transcription." Effective Secretarial Education.
    Reston, Va.: NBEA, 1974, pp. 5—12.

Bulletins, Pamphlets, or Monographs

Pullis, Joe M. Methods of Teaching Shorthand: A Research
    Analysis. Monograph 126. Cincinnati: South—Western
    Publishing Co., 1973.

Government Publications

U.S. Superintendent of Documents, comp. Checklist of United
    States Public Documents, 1789—1909. Vol. I of Lists of
    Congressional and Departmental Publications, 3d ed.,
    rev. and enl. Washington: U.S. Government Printing Of-
    fice, 1911.

Journal/Magazine Article—with Author

Lambrecht, Judith J. "Aptitude Testing in Shorthand." Busi-
    ness Education Forum (October, 1972), pp. 17—24.

Journal/Magazine Article—No Author

"Air Thermometers." <u>Consumer Reports</u> (February, 1966), pp. 74–75.

Newspaper

<u>New York Times</u>, January 15, 1981, p. 3a.

Paperback

Molloy, John T. <u>The Woman's Dress for Success Book</u>. New York: Warner Books, Inc., 1977.

Unpublished Dissertation

Stoddard, Ted Dee. "An Experimental Study in the Utilization of Staff and Equipment for the Teaching of Intermediate Collegiate Shorthand." Doctoral dissertation, Arizona State University, 1967.

FOOTNOTE FORMAT

1114 **Book—One Author**

[1] Franklin Bobbit, <u>How to Make a Curriculum</u> (Boston: Houghton–Mifflin Company, 1924), pp. 107–12.

Book—Repeating Author

[2] Franklin Bobbit, <u>Curriculum and Instruction</u> (Boston: Houghton–Mifflin Company, 1926), p. 118.

Book—Two Authors

[3] Herbert J. Klausmeier and William Goodwin, <u>Learning and Human Abilities</u> (New York: Harper & Row, Publishers, 1966), pp. 228–35.

Book—More Than Three Authors

[4] Lawrence Hall, et al., <u>New Colleges for New Students</u> (San Francisco: Jossey–Bass Inc., Publishers, 1974), p. 97.

Book—with Editor

[5] Charles E. Skinner (ed.), <u>Educational Psychology</u> (New York: Prentice–Hall, 1951), p. 45.

Book—Chapter Reference

[6] Joe M. Pullis, "Variables Affecting Achievement in Shorthand and Transcription," Effective Secretarial Education (Reston, Va.: NBEA, 1974), pp. 5–12.

Bulletins, Pamphlets, or Monographs

[7] Joe M. Pullis, Methods of Teaching Shorthand: A Research Analysis, Monograph 126 (Cincinnati: South-Western Publishing Co., 1973), p. 14.

Government Publications

[8] U.S. Superintendent of Documents, comp., Checklist of United States Public Documents, 1789–1909, Vol. I of Lists of Congressional and Departmental Publications, 3d ed., rev. and enl. (Washington: U.S. Government Printing Office, 1911), pp. 1655–66.

Journal/Magazine Article—with Author

[9] Judith J. Lambrecht, "Aptitude Testing in Shorthand," Business Education Forum (October, 1972), pp. 17–24.

Journal/Magazine Article—No Author

[10] "Air Thermometers," Consumer Reports (February, 1966), pp. 74–75.

Newspaper

[11] Editorial, New York Times, January 15, 1981, p. 3a.

Paperback

[12] John T. Molloy, The Woman's Dress for Success Book (New York: Warner Books, Inc., 1977), p. 18.

Unpublished Dissertation

[13] Ted Dee Stoddard, "An Experimental Study in the Utilization of Staff and Equipment for the Teaching of Intermediate Collegiate Shorthand" (Doctoral dissertation, Arizona State University, 1967), p. 18.

1115   Repeated Footnote References

When a footnote refers to exactly the same source as the previous footnote, the abbreviation *ibid.* (in the same place) can be used.

[14] Ibid.

When a footnote refers to a work by an author fully cited previously (but not the one immediately preceding), a shortened form for the footnote, including simply the author's surname and the reference page number, can be used.

¹⁵Douglas, p. 81.

More formal styles use the abbreviation *loc. cit.* (in the place cited) and *op. cit.* (in the work cited) for subsequent references.

¹⁶Douglas, loc. cit.   (when reference is made to the same page in the work previously identified)

¹⁷Douglas, op. cit., p. 77.   (when reference is made to a different page in the work previously cited)

1116   Citations

A newer form of footnote is called a *citation*. In the citation form of reference, the quoted material is referenced within the report with just the author's surname and the date of publication.

...important when we deal with children." (Myers, 1972)

The bibliographical reference is similar to what it would be in the traditional bibliography, with the addition of the exact page number of the quoted material.

Myers, Jerome L. Fundamentals of Experimental Design. Boston: Allyn and Bacon, Inc., 1972, p. 5.

In the citation form, works by the same author are identified by the difference in the year of publication. Should quoted material include sources by the same author written within the same year, one reference would read "(Smith, 1925A)" and the second "(Smith, 1925B)."

UNIT 12

Envelopes · Mail · Telephone

INCOMING MAIL

1201   In a relatively small firm, the mail carrier may simply drop the mail at a designated spot—perhaps at the desk of a certain secretary. In a firm of medium size, there is usually a mail room of some kind in which work associated with the mail is done. In a large firm, the mail department is usually *centralized* to provide a number of services for other departments in the firm.

1202   Sorting, Delivering, and Opening the Mail

Within the firm, the mail is usually sorted and delivered before it is opened. In some large firms, the mail is opened and sorted in the mail department. If there is enough mail, an electric letter opener may be used.

Regardless of *where* the mail is opened, care should be exercised to avoid discarding any envelope that may contain a needed return address, postmark, date, etc.

1203   Dating Incoming Mail

A time-recording machine or a date stamp may be used to record the time, or the date, or both on incoming documents. This procedure can be useful in establishing dates in matters of law, contracts, etc. It may also be useful in controlling the flow of correspondence.

1204   Inspecting Incoming Mail

Incoming mail should be inspected to determine that

● Noted enclosures are actually included.

194

- All enclosures are noted.

- Return address is on the letter as well as the envelope.

Any discrepancy between the enclosure notation and what is actually in the piece of mail should also be noted on the document.

1205   Retrieving Files

A letter that is part of a familiar routine (orders, payments, a series of letters on any subject, etc.) may call for retrieving a related file *before* the letter is delivered within the office. Delivering the letter and the file related to it *together* saves time and effort.

1206   Routing Slips

Mail that should be circulated to several persons can be controlled with a routing slip. If a piece of mail is to be routed to more than three or four persons, or if it is urgent, the piece should be photocopied. For an example of a routing slip, see Illustration 12-1.

ILLUSTRATION 12-1

Sample Routing Slip

```
    Albert Martin, Director
    Public Relations Department

                         Date 3/25/--

        ROUTING SLIP
                                   Date
                                 Forwarded
        _____ Everyone         _____
        _____ Babb, B.
          ✓  Gryder, H.          3/25
        _____ Igo, J.
        _____ Mundt, K.
          ✓  Primrose, N.        3/25
          ✓  Roehr, P.           3/28
        _____ Slaughter, G.
          ✓  Tucker, C.          3/28
        _____ Wingfield, M.
          ✓  Brown, M.           3/28

    Will you please:

        _____ Read and keep
        _____ Read and pass on
        _____ Read and return
          ✓  Read, pass on, and return
```

12

1207   Recording Incoming Mail

Whether or not all mail is processed by a centralized mail department, a firm may choose to record *some* incoming mail—and perhaps some outgoing mail. Mail in the following categories is typical of the kinds of correspondence frequently recorded:

- Mail between the home office and branch offices.

- Mail between parent firm and subsidiary.

- Correspondence with government agencies.

- Correspondence pertaining to some (or all) law cases.

- Insured mail.

- Special delivery mail.

- Registered and certified mail.

If the firm or office records incoming or outgoing mail, the record will look something like Illustration 12-2.

ILLUSTRATION 12-2

Sample Mail Record

DATE OF ENTRY	ARTICLE	FROM WHOM	DATE SENT	DEPARTMENT	INDIVIDUAL	DATE RECEIVED
9-5	Book	Welch Bros.	9-3		A. Ward	9-6
9-12	Folders	Hill Supply	9-10	Filing		9-14
9-23	Report	Lehman & Cole	9-21	Research		9-25
10-1	Catalog	Tate Mfg. Co.	9-30	Purchasing		10-4
10-3	Tickets	Jack Wylie	10-1		H. Lewis	

1208   High-Priority Correspondence

It is inappropriate to use the routing slip for high-priority correspondence. To do so would be to depend on hand-to-hand transmission within the firm. Since the important thing is to get the correspondence to the person for whom it is intended while making anyone else concerned aware that the correspondence has been received or sent, one of the following methods may be used:

- Have a rubber stamp made to route and control high-priority documents. (See Illustration 12-3.)

ILLUSTRATION 12-3

Rubber Stamp for Routing
High-Priority Correspondence

Date received	File
Document	
From	
Routed to	
Response required by	
The person to whom this document is routed is responsible for the response as indicated.	

- Register high-priority correspondence in the office and add a check-off column to the registry book. Look over the last few pages of the registry book from time to time to make sure none of the registered pieces is outstanding. See ¶ 1207.

- Use a tickler file to remind you when a response is due.

1209 Coding Incoming Correspondence

If centralized files are used, the recording of incoming correspondence may include coding for filing purposes. See ¶ 1207 for recording.

1210 Mail Expected Under Separate Cover

Whether or not other mail is recorded, some firms keep a record of mail expected under separate cover. They do so to make sure that all the pieces of a mailing (letter and package, several packages, etc.) reach the addressee. This record also triggers a follow-up when an expected piece does not arrive.

OUTGOING MAIL

1211 First-Class Mail

First-class mail is delivered by the fastest transportation available. It consists of the following:

- Letters and other material sealed in envelopes or otherwise sealed against postal inspection.

- Postal cards.

- Business reply cards and envelopes.

- Greeting cards.

- Handwritten or typewritten reports, manuscripts, etc. This category includes material that is *partially* handwritten or typewritten and partially printed: bills, checks, money orders, etc.

1212   Priority Mail

First-class mail over 12 ounces is called *priority mail*. It moves by the fastest transportation available and receives the best handling. Priority mail

- Consists of first-class mail over 12 ounces.

- Can weigh no more than 70 pounds.

- Does not exceed 100 inches in combined length and girth. (See Illustration 12-4.)

ILLUSTRATION 12-4

Package Length and Girth Diagram

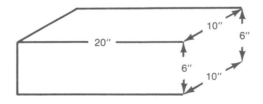

```
Girth: 10 + 6 + 10 + 6 =    32
Length:                     20
Combined Length
& Girth:                    52
```

1213   Minimum Size Limitations

To be mailable, letters, cards, etc., must be at least

- .007 inch thick. This is about the thickness of a postal card. *Thinner pieces are not mailable*.

- 3½ inches high. Pieces less than 3½ inches high *are not mailable*.

- 5 inches long. Pieces shorter than 5 inches *are not mailable*.

1214   Minimum-Weight, Odd-Size Surcharge on Some First-Class Mail

A special surcharge is levied on first-class mail *weighing one ounce or less and exceeding*

* 6 ⅛ inches high, *or*
* 11 ½ inches long, *or*
* ¼ inch thick.

Odd-shaped pieces *weighing one ounce or less* are subject to the same surcharge.

Note: Minimum size standards are used to make machine processing easier. The surcharge is to pay for hand processing, which is more expensive than machine processing.

1215   Second-Class Mail

Second-class mail is for certain newspapers and magazines. Those that meet the requirements of the Postal Service for second-class mail may be sent at rates lower than those for third-class mail or parcel mail. There are separate second-class categories for individual copies of newspapers and magazines and for bulk mailings (multiple copies of the same publication).

1216   Minimum-Weight, Odd-Size Surcharge on Some Second-Class Mail

A special surcharge is levied on second-class mail *weighing two ounces or less and exceeding*

* 6⅛ inches high, *or*
* 11½ inches long, *or*
* ¼ inch thick.

Odd-size second-class mail *weighing two ounces or less* is subject to the same surcharge.

1217   Third-Class Mail

Third-class mail consists primarily of advertising material. It may be used for any printed material, as well as other kinds of merchandise. Third-class mail

* Must weigh less than 16 ounces.

- May be used by anyone, but is used more for large mailings than for individual pieces.

- Employs two rate structures: *single pieces* (one-of-a-kind or one-at-a-time) and *bulk* (multiple mailing—batches of identical pieces).

- Accommodates sealed envelopes if they are marked "Third Class" on the address side of the envelope. Otherwise, sealed envelopes are *processed* as first-class mail and *billed* as first-class mail.

1218   Fourth-Class Mail (Parcel Post)

Fourth-class mail is used for packages *weighing 16 ounces or more*. With fourth-class mail

- There are maximums on size and weight.

- Heavier packages are more costly to send.

- It is more costly to send packages to *distant* zones.

- Packages may be sent sealed or unsealed. Unless they are sent first-class—and marked that way—packages are usually processed fourth-class.

- Priority mail (¶ 1212) or express mail (¶ 1219) may be used for faster service over long distances.

1219   Express Mail

Express mail service is for the postal customer who wants fast, reliable, overnight service. It is available at larger post offices. If express mail is not delivered overnight, the Postal Service refunds the postage.

1220   Special Delivery

Special delivery mail

- May be obtained for all classes of mail.

- Provides for delivery during certain specified hours that include and extend beyond regular business hours.

- Is delivered on Sundays and holidays.

- May be sent to post offices served by city mail carriers and to smaller post offices not so served if the destination lies within a one-mile radius of the destination post office.

- Speeds the movement of mail, but does not guarantee delivery by special messenger.

1221   Certificate of Mailing

A certificate of mailing may be obtained at a nominal fee. It proves that you mailed something but does not provide insurance against loss or damage.

1222   Certified Mail

Certified mail

- Provides you with a mailing receipt.

- Moves as ordinary mail—receives no special care.

- Provides (for an extra fee) a return receipt proving that the article was delivered.

- Is not for valuable articles. Valuable articles should be sent by insured mail or registered mail.

1223   Return Receipts

A return receipt

- Is proof of delivery.

- Is available for insured mail valued at more than $15, certified mail, registered mail, and c.o.d. mail.

- Allows you to place certain restrictions on who receives the article and provides you with additional information about the delivery—if you request the additional service and pay for it at the time of mailing.

1224   Insurance

Insurance, in amounts to $400, is available on

- Parcel post.

- Third-class mail.

- Priority mail.

- First-class mail.

1225   Registered Mail

Articles that cannot be replaced and those valued at $400 or more should be sent registered mail. With registered mail

- Insurance up to $25,000 on all domestic (inside the United States) deliveries is included in the registration fee.

- You must declare the full value of the article(s) mailed at the time of mailing.

- You receive a receipt at the time of mailing.

- The mail is controlled during its movement from you to the addressee.

- For an extra fee, you receive a return receipt telling you to whom, when, and where your registered mail was delivered.

SPECIAL POSTAL SERVICES

1226 Collect (or Cash) on Delivery Service (c.o.d.)

Anyone can send a package c.o.d. If you sold something to someone and wanted the Postal Service to deliver it and collect the money for you, you would send the article c.o.d. The Postal Service would collect the selling price you specified, plus the postage, plus the c.o.d. fee and return that amount to you in the form of a postal money order. Mail sent c.o.d. can be registered and insured.

1227 Money Orders

Postal money orders for payment in the United States may be purchased at any post office in amounts up to $400. If a money order is lost or stolen, it can be replaced. Copies of paid money orders can be obtained for two years after the date of payment. Most *large* post offices can arrange money order payments in foreign nations.

1228 Forwarding Mail

Before you move, obtain a change of address kit from your post office. It contains the materials and instructions for notifying the Postal Service of your plans, as well as cards for notifying all those with whom you correspond.

1229 Postal Service Manual

Postal laws, regulations, services, and rates change from time to time. It is a good idea to have a copy of the *Postal Service Manual* in the office. It is available from or through your post office.

PREPARING MAIL FOR THE POSTAL SERVICE

1230 Addressing Envelopes

Of the two forms shown in Illustrations 12-5 and 12-6 for envelopes, the Postal Service prefers the all capital, no punctuation form.

ILLUSTRATION 12-5

Small Envelope

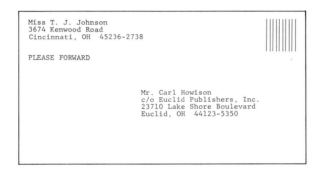

ILLUSTRATION 12-6

Large Envelope

Return address. If the return address of your firm is printed on the envelope, type above the return address the name of the person who is sending the mail. This is not done in mass mailings.

Address. Begin the address seven spaces to the left of the horizontal center of the envelope and on line 12 of a small envelope or line 14 of a large envelope.

Nine-digit ZIP Code. The U.S. Postal Service expects to add four more digits to the standard five-digit ZIP Code. The expanded ZIP Code will enable the Postal Service to assign one 9-digit number to each recipient of large amounts of mail in the current postal ZIP areas. An example of the new usage might be:

> Franklin Paper Company
> 1501 Madison Road
> Cincinnati, OH   45227-1010
> (Hypothetical nine-digit code)

Note: See ¶ 1008 for more information on using ZIP Codes.

Envelope notations. *Addressee* notations, such as PERSONAL or PLEASE FORWARD, intended for the recipient or someone who handles mail for the recipient are typed in all capital letters a triple space below the return address and three spaces from the left edge of the envelope. (See Illustration 12-7.)

Mailing notations, such as REGISTERED and SPECIAL DELIVERY, intended for Postal Service personnel should be typed a triple space below the postage stamp or postage meter mark. Type the notation in all capital letters. See Illustration 12-8 for information on choosing envelopes and folding letters.

1231   Addressing Machines

A firm that uses machine-processed address plates for mass mailings keeps a plate for each addressee. The plate is made of metal or plastic and is similar in size and appearance to a plastic credit card.

Some addressing machine systems permit the plates to be coded for the selection of predetermined groups of addressees (customers, suppliers, prospects, certain geographic areas, etc.). The machine will select those plates that have the predetermined code and reject those that do not.

1232   Stencils and Gummed Label Duplication

Machines that process special small stencils in a manner similar to that of addressing machines are also available.

Mailing lists also may be typed on full-size stencils, offset masters, or spirit masters, and run on sheets of pressure-sensitive gummed labels. In the absence of specialized addressing machines, this method is particularly effective when repeated mailings are made to the same group of addressees because a duplicator run will provide enough labels for several mailings. Even

ILLUSTRATION 12-7

Envelopes with Notations

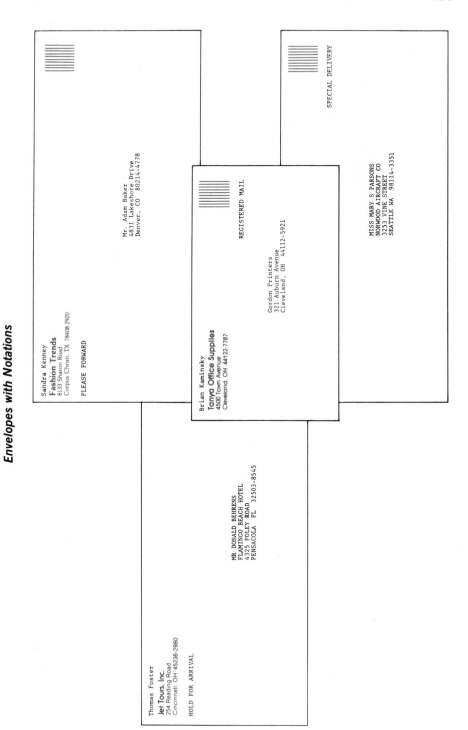

Sandra Kenney
Fashion Trends
8133 Sharon Road
Corpus Christi, TX 78408 2920

PLEASE FORWARD

Mr. Adam Baker
4831 Lakeshore Drive
Denver, CO 80214-4778

Brian Kaminsky
Tanya Office Supplies
4500 Town Avenue
Cleveland, OH 44122-7787

REGISTERED MAIL

Gordon Printers
321 Auburn Avenue
Cleveland, OH 44112-5921

SPECIAL DELIVERY

MISS MARY S PARSONS
NORWOOD AIRCRAFT CO
3253 VINE STREET
SEATTLE WA 98114-3351

Thomas Foster
Jet Tours, Inc.
254 Reading Road
Cincinnati. OH 45236-2980

HOLD FOR ARRIVAL

MR DONALD BEHRENS
FLAMINGO BEACH HOTEL
4325 FOLEY ROAD
PENSACOLA FL 32503-8545

ILLUSTRATION 12-8

Choosing Envelopes and Folding Letters

Stationery	Envelope	Fold	Window Envelope Fold
Standard (8½″ x 11″)	No. 10 (9½″ x 4⅛″) No. 6¾ (6½″ x 3⅝″)	3 2-3	W3 —
Monarch (7¼″ x 10½″)	No. 7 (7½″ x 3⅞″)	3	W3
Baronial (5½″ x 8½″)	No. 6¾ (6½″ x 3⅝″) No. 5⅜ (5¹⁵/₁₆″ x 4⅝″)	3 2	W3 W2

Fold 2	 Fold into 2 parts.
Fold 2-3	 Fold into 2 parts, then fold into 3 parts.
Fold 3	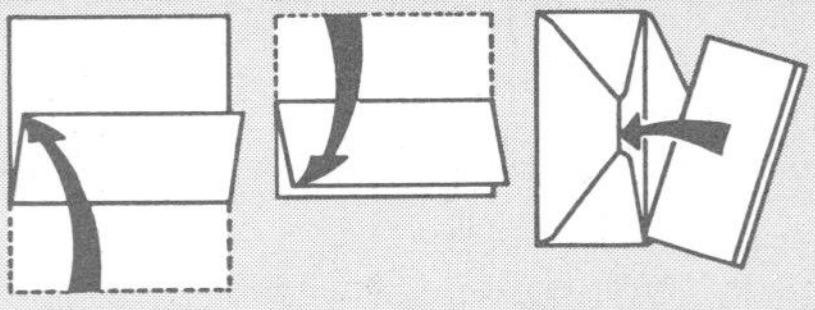
Fold W2 **(Window** **Envelope)**	 Fold into 2 parts.
Fold W3 **(Window** **Envelope)**	 Fold into 3 parts.

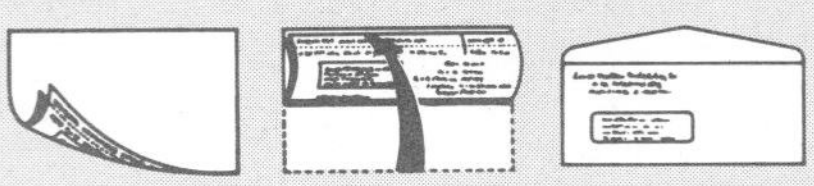

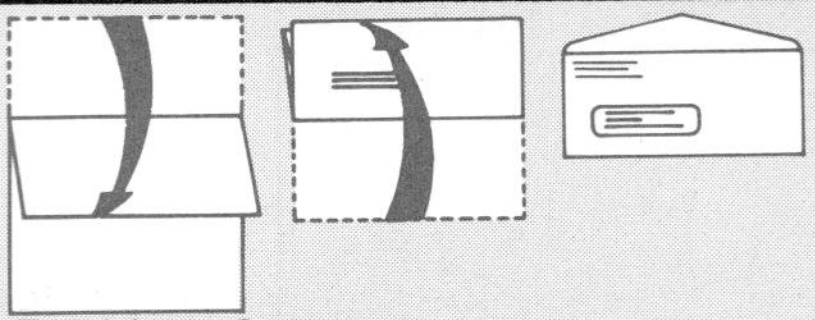

if multiple copies of the address list are not needed, pressure-sensitive labels are useful in mailing packages or envelopes that will not fit a typewriter. The labels are typed, then applied to the package or envelope.

1233   Computer Addressing

Mailing lists may be stored in a computer and then run—the whole list, or selected parts of the list. The address list may also be stored on punched cards, magnetic tape, magnetic discs, etc., and fed into the computer as needed. In addition to printing the names, addresses, etc., the computer can select certain addresses and reject others without destroying the order of the list. The computer can print on continuous sheets of pressure-sensitive gummed labels or directly on special envelopes that are manufactured in continuous form.

1234   Business Reply Mail

Your post office can issue a permit to use business reply cards and envelopes. The card or envelope is enclosed in your outgoing mail—perhaps a sales letter. The addressee may then use the card or envelope to respond to you. The person responding does not have to address the card or envelope (your address is printed on it) or pay the postage. You will pay a little more than regular postage because of handling costs when the card or letter is returned to you. You pay postage only on cards and letters you receive—not on those that are sent out but are not returned. Illustration 12-9 shows an example of a business reply card.

1235   International Mail

If you mail material to foreign nations infrequently, the best procedure is to ask your post office for assistance as the need arises. If you mail such material frequently, a copy of *The Directory of International Mail* may be helpful.

Canada and Mexico. Rates for letters and postal cards sent to Canada and Mexico are the same as those employed for *domestic mail* (mail within the United States).

Letters and cards. *"LC mail"* rates depend on the destination and weight. LC mail is subject to size restrictions and weight maximums that vary from nation to nation.

Parcel post. Other articles (packages) may be mailed at international parcel post rates. Parcel post rates are lower than those for letters and cards.

ILLUSTRATION 12-9

Business Reply Card

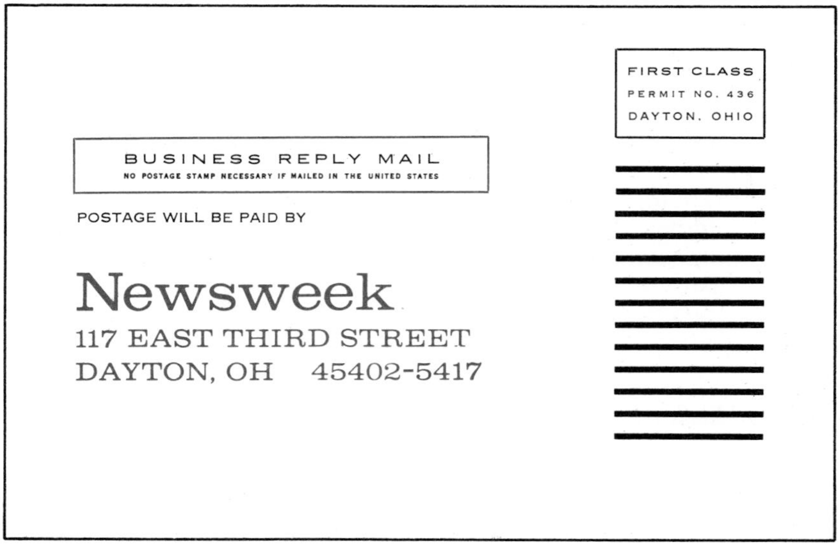

Because rates and regulations vary from nation to nation, most people will call their post offices each time a parcel is mailed— especially if special services are desirable or special regulations apply. When mailing internationally:

• Most packages can be registered.

• Most packages can be insured.

• C.o.d. service is *not* generally available.

• Special handling service *is* generally available.

• Customs declarations are required for most packages.

• Business reply (return postage paid) coupons may be used, subject to international regulations.

• Airmail is generally available, including international air parcel post.

THE TELEPHONE

1236   Telephone Service

The telephone directory. The *telephone directory* contains information on most of the following topics. These brief descriptions are intended to help you understand the services available from your telephone company.

Directory Assistance. *Directory Assistance* formerly was called "Information." This service supplies telephone numbers and other information helpful in placing calls. Directory Assistance should be used only for information not in the telephone directory. Many telephone companies are now charging for this service.

1237   Types of Telephone Calls

Person-to-person calls. *Person-to-person calls* enable you to call a specific person or extension telephone. You are not charged unless you reach the person or telephone you are calling.

Collect calls. A *collect call* is a long-distance telephone call where the receiver (or called party) accepts the charges.

Credit card calls. You can charge your calls to a credit card issued by your telephone company.

Third-number calls. You can charge a call to a third number. This service is particularly useful when you are away from home and wish to place a long-distance call to a number other than your home telephone number. You can charge the call to your home telephone.

Coin calls. Instructions for placing coin calls are posted on the pay telephone.

Conference calls. You can talk with three or more people in different places at the same time. The numbers you call for a conference can be all local, all long distance, or mixed. Tell the operator you want to place a conference call.

1238   Special Services; Long Distance

Time and charges. When a long-distance call is completed, the operator will, if requested to do so, tell you the time you talked and the amount of the charges.

WATS numbers. Some firms maintain Wide Area Telecommunications Service for their customers and others who they want to call them. The firm that purchases WATS service pays by the month.

You do not pay for calls you make on WATS lines maintained by others. These "free" lines are usually in the 1-800 series.

Long-distance Directory Assistance. If you need Directory Assistance outside your own area code, dial 1, plus the area code of the city you wish to reach, plus 555-1212.

Overseas calls. Some telephones in some cities are equipped for direct dialing to foreign nations. See the instructions in your telephone directory or call the operator.

Long-distance rates. Long-distance rates vary significantly by time of day. See your telephone directory for information on timing your calls to save money. Be aware of differences in time zones when placing long-distance calls. A 9:00 a.m. call made from New York would be received at 6:00 a.m. in California.

THE TELEGRAPH

1239   Telegrams

A telegraph message may be sent by

- Full-rate telegram.
- Overnight telegram.
- Mailgram.
- International full-rate telegram.
- International letter.

Full-rate telegram. A *full-rate telegram*

- Is the fastest and most expensive service.
- Is usually delivered within a few hours.
- Is accepted anytime (24 hours a day).
- Carries a minimum charge for 15 words.

Overnight telegram. For an *overnight telegram*

- The message is accepted until midnight and is delivered the following morning or very early in the afternoon.
- The minimum charge is for 100 words.

Mailgram. A *mailgram* is

● Accepted anytime of the day or night.

● Sent electronically to a post office teleprinter at a post office near the destination.

● Usually delivered in the next day's mail.

● Billed with a minimum charge for 100 words.

● Available before the next day's mail if the subscriber maintains a post office box and has mailgrams addressed to the post office box.

1240   International Telegrams

International service. International telegraphic communications take place between nations by *cablegram* when the nations are connected by cable and by *radiogram* when cable connections are unavailable. Radiograms can also reach aircraft, ships, and trains.

International full-rate telegram. The *international full-rate telegram*, similar to the domestic full-rate telegram, is the faster and more expensive international telegram. It may travel by radio or cable.

International letter telegram. The *international letter telegram* accommodates longer messages at lower rates. The service is slower (overnight); international letter telegrams travel by radio or cable.

1241   Telegram Forms

Western Union provides blank forms on which messages may be handwritten or typewritten. Typewritten messages are preferred. They should be double-spaced and typed in capital and lowercase letters. This makes the message easier to read. There is no need to copy the all-capital format of teleprinters. Do not divide words at the ends of lines.

Some firms prefer to have their own telegram forms printed. Most people think either type of printed form is better than blank paper or letterheads because it immediately identifies the message as a telegram and the check-off lists (rate, type of service, etc.) save time.

1242   Confirmation Copy

For an additional fee, Western Union will mail a confirmation copy of the telegram to the addressee. As an alternative, the sender may wish to mail a confirmation copy that will arrive after the telegram message has been delivered by Western Union.

1243   Hand Delivery

For an additional fee, Western Union will have a messenger hand-deliver the message.

Proof of delivery. When a message is to be hand delivered, the sender can request a receipt to be signed by the addressee certifying that the message has been delivered.

1244   Hardware

Many hardware devices are used to provide the services described in ¶¶ 1239-43, as well as some additional related services:

- **Teleprinter.** The *teleprinter* is installed in the offices of users. The operator "types" the message on the teleprinter; the message is received (typewritten) in the telegraph office. Messages are received as the Western Union operator types the message.

- **Telex.** *Telex* is a teletypewriter network owned by Western Union. It connects subscribers to the network via teletypewriter anytime of the day or night, permitting quick access to other Telex subscribers, immediate transmission/reception (not through a Western Union office), and hard-copy accuracy.

- **TWX.** *TWX* is another teletypewriter network similar to Telex, also owned by Western Union. Telex and TWX subscribers can communicate with each other.

- **Microwave transmission.** A series of towers and relay stations connect major cities via microwave equipment that transmits voice, data, pictures, etc., via microwave (ultra short wave length) radio beams.

- **Satellite transmission.** Satellite service may be purchased to relay transmissions across the nation or to and from distant parts of the world.

- **Data transmission.** Each year, more firms increase the sophistication of their own communications systems. From relatively simple networks of teleprinters to computers that "talk to each other," the use of data transmission systems is expanding rapidly. All the equipment described in this section is used as part of or in conjunction with those systems.

1245   Special Services

Western Union provides certain special services:

- **Money orders.** The sender pays a local Western Union office; Western Union pays through almost any telegraph office in the world.

- **Messenger service.** Messengers may be hired to run errands, such as delivering parcels, hard-copy messages, etc.

- **Reservations.** Reservations for transportation and lodging can be made easily and efficiently by wire.

- **Special greetings.** Special greetings for birthdays, holidays, etc., are available through local Western Union offices.

- **Merchandise.** Gifts (candy, flowers, etc.) can be "sent" by wire.

You may be interested in additional information on some of the items discussed in this manual. Additional references are provided below. This listing offers specialized sources to help you solve typical office questions and problems. Ask for the latest edition in ordering. Many of the items listed will be found in your local public library.

ALMANACS

1301   Almanacs are usually published on an annual basis and contain up-to-date information on historical, economic, social, and political facts. Yearly updated almanacs provide useful information on the previous year's happenings, such as election statistics, athletic events and records, names of government officials, memorable dates and holidays, etc.

> *Information Please Almanac, Atlas, and Yearbook.* New York: Simon & Schuster, Inc.
> *The Official Associated Press Almanac.* Maplewood, NJ: Hammond, Inc.
> *Reader's Digest Almanac and Yearbook.* New York: W. W. Norton & Co., Inc.
> *The World Almanac and Book of Facts.* New York: Doubleday & Co., Inc.

BIOGRAPHICAL REFERENCES

13

1302   Biographical references are handy sources of information on prominent women and men. Data provided include age, education, occupation or profession, marital status, affiliations, honors, and achievements.

Current Biography. New York: The H. W. Wilson Company.
Dictionary of American Biography. New York: Charles Scribner's Sons.
Official Congressional Directory. Washington, D. C.: United States Government Printing Office.
Webster's Biographical Dictionary. Springfield, MA: G. & C. Merriam Company.
Who's Who. New York: St. Martin's Press, Inc.
Who's Who in America. Chicago: Marquis Who's Who, Inc.
Who's Who in American Women. Chicago: Marquis Who's Who, Inc.
Who's Who in Commerce and Industry. Chicago: Marquis Who's Who, Inc.
Who's Who in the East. Chicago: Marquis Who's Who, Inc.
Who's Who in the Midwest. Chicago: Marquis Who's Who, Inc.
Who's Who in the South and Southwest. Chicago: Marquis Who's Who, Inc.
Who's Who in the West. Chicago: Marquis Who's Who, Inc.

BOOKS AND PERIODICAL REFERENCES

1303   The references listed below provide up-to-date information on the latest books and periodicals published in each subject category. If your employer subscribes to a large number of magazines or periodicals, file a photocopy of the table of contents page before storing the publication. This will make it easier to retrieve any particular article as needed.

Ayer Directory of Publications. Philadelphia: Ayer Press.
Books in Print, U.S.A.: An Index to the Publishers Trade List Annual. New York: R. R. Bowker Company.
Business Education Index. New York: Delta Pi Epsilon Fraternity and Gregg Division/McGraw-Hill Book Company.
Business Periodicals Index. New York: The H. W. Wilson Company.
Cumulative Book Index. New York: The H. W. Wilson Company.
Education Index. New York: The H. W. Wilson Company.
The New York Times Index. New York: The New York Times.
The Publishers' Trade List Annual. New York: R. R. Bowker Company.
Reader's Guide to Periodical Literature. New York: The H. W. Wilson Company.

BUSINESS, FINANCIAL, AND CREDIT REFERENCES

13

1304   Business, financial, and credit references provide current information on businesses and professions and the people who work in them.

American Medical Directory. Chicago: American Medical Association.

Dun & Bradstreet Ratings and Reports. New York: Dun &
Bradstreet, Inc.

Encyclopedia of Associations. Detroit: Gale Research Co.

Fortune Directory. New York: *Fortune* Magazine.

The Martindale-Hubbell Law Directory. Summit, NJ:
Martindale-Hubbell, Inc.

Polk's World Bank Directory, North American Edition. Nashville:
R. L. Polk & Co.

Rand McNally International Bankers Directory. Chicago: Rand
McNally & Company.

Standard Corporation Records. New York: Standard & Poor's
Corp.

Thomas Register of American Manufacturers. New York:
Thomas Publishing Company.

DICTIONARIES AND WORDBOOKS

1305   One of the most important general references for the office
worker, the dictionary (and various wordbooks), is published in
various sizes, from pocket-size to large volumes. Abridged dictionaries provide information about most common words, while
unabridged dictionaries contain information on almost every word
in the English language. Wordbooks are useful sources for spelling
and word division of specialized vocabulary. Remember to check
the spelling of any word you are uncertain of.

The American College Dictionary. New York: Random House,
Inc.

The American Heritage Dictionary of the English Language.
Boston: American Heritage Publishing Co., Inc. and
Houghton-Mifflin Company.

Anderson, Ruth I., Lura Lynn Straub, and E. Dana Gibson. *Word
Finder.* Englewood Cliffs, NJ: Prentice-Hall.

Brown, Alvin R. *Spelling: A Mnemonics Approach.* Cincinnati:
South-Western Publishing Co.

Byers, Edward E. *10,000 Medical Words.* New York: Gregg
Division/McGraw-Hill Book Company.

Funk & Wagnall's Standard College Dictionary. New York:
Harcourt Brace Jovanovich, Inc.

How and Where to Look It Up. New York: McGraw-Hill Book
Company.

Kahn, Gilbert, and Donald J. D. Mulkerne. *The Word Book.*
Beverly Hills: Glencoe Press.

Lamb, Marion M. *Word Studies.* Cincinnati: South-Western Publishing Co.

Leslie, Louis A. *20,000 Words*. New York: Gregg Division/ McGraw-Hill Book Company.

Kurtz, Margaret A. *10,000 Legal Words*. New York: Gregg Division/McGraw-Hill Book Company.

The Random House Dictionary of the English Language. New York: Random House, Inc.

Roget's International Thesaurus of Words and Phrases. New York: Crowell Collier and Macmillan, Inc.

The Original Roget's Thesaurus of English Words and Phrases. New York: St. Martin's Press, Inc.

Silverthorn, J. E., and Devern J. Perry. *Word Division Manual*. Cincinnati: South-Western Publishing Co.

Sisson, A. F. *Sisson's Word and Expression Locator*. West Nyack, NY: Parker Publishing Company.

Webster's New Collegiate Dictionary. Springfield, MA: G. & C. Merriam Company.

Webster's New Dictionary of Synonyms. Springfield, MA: G. & C. Merriam Company.

Webster's New World Dictionary of the American Language. New York: World Publishing Co.

Webster's Third New International Dictionary of the English Language. Springfield, MA: G. & C. Merriam Company.

ENCYCLOPEDIAS

1306   Encyclopedias are usually multiple volumes arranged alphabetically. Each volume contains a variety of information on a great many subjects. In addition, encyclopedias are illustrated with pictures, graphs, charts, and maps to aid the reader.

Encyclopedia Americana. New York: Americana Corporation.

Lincoln Library of Essential Information. Buffalo: Frontier Press Company.

The New Columbia Encyclopedia. New York: Columbia University Press.

The New Encyclopaedia Britannica. Chicago: Encyclopaedia Britannica, Inc.

The New York Times Encyclopedic Almanac. New York: The New York Times Co., Book Division.

PERSONAL/SOCIAL DEVELOPMENT

1307   Eggland, Steven A., and John W. Williams. *Human Relations in Business*. Cincinnati: South-Western Publishing Co.

Post, Emily. *Emily Post's Etiquette*. New York: Funk & Wagnalls, Inc.

Reynolds, Caroline. *Dimensions in Personal Development*. Cincinnati: South-Western Publishing Co.
Vanderbilt, Amy. *Amy Vanderbilt's Complete Book of Etiquette*. New York: Doubleday & Co., Inc.
Vermes, J. *Complete Book of Business Etiquette*. West Nyack, NY: Parker Publishing Company.

GEOGRAPHICAL, POSTAL, SHIPPING, AND TRAVEL INFORMATION

1308   *Address Abbreviations*. Washington, D. C.: U. S. Postal Service Publication No. 59, U. S. Government Printing Office.
Bullinger's Postal and Shippers Guide for the United States, Canada, and Newfoundland. Westwood, NJ: Bullinger's Guides, Inc.
Customs Regulations of the United States. Washington, D. C.: Superintendent of Documents, U. S. Government Printing Office.
Hotel and Motel Red Book. New York: American Hotel Association Directory.
National ZIP Code Directory. Washington, D. C.: U. S. Government Printing Office.
Official Airline Guide. Sausalito, CA: Official Airline Guide.
The Postal Manual. Washington, D. C: Superintendent of Documents, U. S. Government Printing Office.
Rand McNally Commercial Atlas and Marketing Guide. Chicago: Rand McNally & Company.
Rand McNally New Cosmopolitan World Atlas. Chicago: Rand McNally & Company.
Vacations U.S.A.–Getting Most for Your Travel Dollar. Washington, D. C.: Kiplinger Washington Editors.

GRAMMAR, STYLE, PUNCTUATION, CAPITALIZATION, AND ABBREVIATION REFERENCES

1309   Brown, Leland. *Communicating Facts and Ideas in Business*. New York: Prentice-Hall.
Burtness, Paul S., and Alfred T. Clark, Jr. *Effective English for Business Communication*. Cincinnati: South-Western Publishing Co.
Campbell, William Giles. *Form and Style in Thesis Writing*. Boston: Houghton-Mifflin Company.
Frailey, L. E. *Handbook of Business Letters*. New York: Prentice-Hall.
Hodges, John C., and Mary E. Whitten. *Harbrace College Handbook*. New York: Harcourt Brace Jovanovich, Inc.

Keithley, Erwin M., and Margaret H. Thompson. *English for Modern Business*. Homewood, IL: Richard D. Irwin, Inc.

A Manual of Style. Chicago: The University of Chicago Press.

Perkins, W. E. *Punctuation: A Programmed Approach*. Cincinnati: South-Western Publishing Co.

Perrin, Porter G. *Writer's Guide and Index to English*. Chicago: Scott, Foresman & Company.

Schachter, Norman, and Alfred T. Clark, Jr. *Basic English Review*. Cincinnati: South-Western Publishing Co.

Schachter, Norman, and Alfred T. Clark, Jr. *English the Easy Way*. Cincinnati: South-Western Publishing Co.

Schwartz, Robert J. *The Complete Dictionary of Abbreviations*. New York: Thomas Y. Crowell Company, Publishers.

Style Manual. Washington, D. C.: U. S. Government Printing Office.

Wolf, Morris P., Dale F. Keyser, and Robert R. Aurner. *Effective Communication in Business*. Cincinnati: South-Western Publishing Co.

JOB SEARCH SOURCES

1310   When you are in the process of looking for a new position, the following job search sources may assist with some additional information.

Figgins, Ross. *Techniques of Job Search*. San Francisco: Canfield Press.

Goble, Dorothy Y. *How to Get a Job and Keep It*. Austin: Steck-Vaughn Company.

Molloy, John T. *Dress for Success*. New York: Warner Books, Inc.

_____. *The Woman's Dress for Success Book*. New York: Warner Books, Inc.

Pivar, William H. *Work Experience Handbook*. San Francisco: Canfield Press.

Resume Service. *Resumes That Get Jobs*. New York: Arco Publishing Co., Inc.

Walter, Tim, and Al Siebert. *Student Success*. New York: Holt, Rinehart & Winston.

QUOTATIONS

1311   Bartlett, John. *Familiar Quotations*. Boston: Little, Brown & Company.

Sisson, A. F. *Sisson's Word and Expression Locator*. West Nyack, NY: Parker Publishing Company.

SECRETARIAL HANDBOOKS

1312   Anderson, Ruth I., Dorothy E. Lee, Allien A. Russon, Jacquelyn A. Wentzell, and Helen M. S. Horack. *The Administrative Secretary: Resource.* New York: Gregg Division/McGraw-Hill Book Company.

Association of Records Managers and Administrators. *Rules for Alphabetical Filing.* Chicago: Association of Records Managers and Administrators.

Bassett, Ernest D., David G. Goodman, and Joseph S. Fosegan. *Business Records Control.* Cincinnati: South-Western Publishing Co.

Becker, Esther R., and Evelyn Anders. *The Successful Secretary's Handbook.* New York: Harper & Row, Publishers.

Clark, James L., Jr., and Lyn R. Clark. *How 2: A Handbook for Office Workers.* Belmont, CA: Wadsworth Publishing Co., Inc.

Doris, Lillian, and Besse May Miller. *Complete Secretary's Handbook.* Englewood Cliffs, NJ: Prentice-Hall.

Engel, Pauline. *Executive Secretary's Handbook.* Englewood Cliffs, NJ: Prentice-Hall.

Flynn, Patricia. *The Complete Secretary.* Belmont, CA: Fearon-Pitman Publishers, Inc.

Hanna, J. Marshall, Estelle L. Popham, and Rita Sloan Tilton. *Secretarial Procedures and Administration.* Cincinnati: South-Western Publishing Co.

Hutchinson, Lois Irene. *Standard Handbook for Secretaries.* New York: Gregg Division/McGraw-Hill Book Company.

Janis, J. Harold, and Margaret H. Thompson. *New Standard Reference for Secretaries and Administrative Assistants.* New York: Macmillan, Inc.

Johnson, Mina M., and Norman F. Kallaus. *Records Management.* Cincinnati: South-Western Publishing Co.

Kabbe, E. *Medical Secretary's Guide.* Englewood Cliffs, NJ: Prentice-Hall.

Kahn, Gilbert, Theodore Yerian, and Jeffrey R. Stewart, Jr., *Filing Systems and Records Management.* New York: McGraw-Hill Book Company.

Lessenberry, D. D., T. James Crawford, Lawrence W. Erickson, Lee R. Beaumont, Jerry W. Robinson. *Century 21 Typewriting.* Cincinnati: South-Western Publishing Co.

Miller, Besse May. *Legal Secretary's Complete Handbook.* Englewood Cliffs, NJ: Prentice-Hall.

Parker Publishing Company Editorial Staff. *155 Office Shortcuts and Time Savers for the Secretary.* West Nyack, NY: Parker Publishing Company.

_____. *Secretary's Desk Book.* West Nyack, NY: Parker Publishing Company.

_____. *The Successful Secretary.* West Nyack, NY: Parker Publishing Company.

Sabin, William A. *Reference Manual for Stenographers and Typists*. New York: Gregg Division/McGraw-Hill Book Company.

Sletwold, E. *Sletwold's Manual of Documents and Forms for the Legal Secretary*. Englewood Cliffs, NJ: Prentice-Hall.

Taintor, Sarah, and Kate M. Monroe. *Secretary's Handbook*. New York: Macmillan, Inc.

Wanous, S. J., C. H. Duncan, S. E. Warner, and T. E. Langford. *College Typewriting*. Cincinnati: South-Western Publishing Co.

Whalen, Doris H. *The Secretary's Handbook*. New York: Harcourt Brace Jovanovich, Inc.

INDEX

Numbers refer to paragraph numbers.

Numbers refer to paragraph numbers.

Numbers refer to paragraph numbers.

Numbers refer to paragraph numbers.

Numbers refer to paragraph numbers.

Numbers refer to paragraph numbers.

Numbers refer to paragraph numbers.

Numbers refer to paragraph numbers.

Numbers refer to paragraph numbers.

Numbers refer to paragraph numbers.

Numbers refer to paragraph numbers.

Contents

By matching up the guides at the edge of this page with the marks opposite them along the edge of the book, you can quickly turn to the unit containing the material you want.